FINANCIAL UNDERDOG

Financial Underdog enables financial inclusion by providing access to professional-grade financial tools and education for free or at a fraction of the cost of a financial advisor. Often the people that need financial advice the most are those that can't afford it, and many who do use professional investment services use them when they could have self-served.

We are passionate about democratising the world of finance and investment. Financial literacy should be accessible to and engaging for everyone.

Follow us at

@financial_underdog

or visit

www.financialunderdog.com

for more information

THE ~~UN~~BIASED INVESTOR

A BOOK BY FINANCIAL UNDERDOG

For the neurodiverse out there, many of whom are not subject to any of these biases!

CONTENTS

INTRODUCTION: THE ~~UN~~BIASED INVESTOR   ix

PART 1   COGNITIVE BIASES

I.	THE ANCHORING EFFECT	1
II.	THE FUNDAMENTAL ATTRIBUTION ERROR	7
III.	THE BACKFIRE EFFECT	13
IV.	THE FRAMING EFFECT	21
V.	APOPHENIA	27
VI.	THE ILLUSION OF CONTROL	33
VII.	PROPORTIONALITY BIAS	39
VIII.	THE NARRATIVE FALLACY	45
IX.	THE GAMBLER'S FALLACY	53
X.	OVERCONFIDENCE BIAS	59
XI.	CONFIRMATION BIAS	63
XII.	REPRESENTATIVE BIAS	67
XIII.	THE CLUSTERING ILLUSION	73
XIV.	HINDSIGHT BIAS	79
XV.	RECENCY BIAS	85
XVI.	SELF-SERVING BIAS	89
XVII.	THE SUNK COST FALLACY	95
XVIII.	THE AVAILABILITY HEURISTIC	101
XIX.	THE IKEA EFFECT	107
XX.	THE DUNNING-KRUGER EFFECT	115
XXI.	NEGATIVITY BIAS	121
XXII.	THE JUST-WORLD FALLACY	127
XXIII.	THE FALSE CONSENSUS EFFECT	133
XXIV.	THE PLACEBO EFFECT	139
XXV.	MENTAL ACCOUNTING	147
XXVI.	THE CURSE OF KNOWLEDGE	153
XXVII.	THE SOCRATIC PARADOX	159
XXVIII.	ZERO-RISK BIAS	163

XXIX.	THE PLANNING FALLACY	169
XXX.	THE ENDOWMENT EFFECT	175
XXXI.	PAREIDOLIA	179
XXXII.	THE CAUSALITY FALLACY	185
XXXIII.	TELEOLOGICAL THINKING	191
XXXIV.	THE HOT HAND FALLACY	197

PART 2 EMOTIONAL BIASES

XXXV.	LOSS AVERSION	207
XXXVI.	THE DISPOSITION EFFECT	213
XXXVII.	THE AFFECT HEURISTIC	219
XXXVIII.	REGRET AVERSION	225

PART 3 SOCIAL BIASES

XXXIX.	THE HALO EFFECT	233
XL.	HERD MENTALITY	239
XLI.	SOCIAL PROOF	245
XLII.	IN-GROUP FAVOURITISM	251
XLIII.	OPTIMISM BIAS	259
XLIV.	REACTANCE	265
XLV.	THE SPOTLIGHT EFFECT	273
XLVI.	THE BYSTANDER EFFECT	281
XLVII.	AUTHORITY BIAS	289
XLVIII.	EGOCENTRIC BIAS	295
XLIX.	STATUS QUO BIAS	301
L.	THE OSTRICH EFFECT	307

CONCLUSION — 313

FURTHER READING — 315

INTRODUCTION: THE ~~UN~~BIASED INVESTOR

Investment decisions are not made in a vacuum. They are influenced by a multitude of factors, including economic indicators, market trends and financial theories. However, one of the most significant yet often overlooked factors influencing investment behaviour is the investor's own psychology. Behavioural finance, a field that combines the insights of psychology with economics, sheds light on how cognitive, emotional and social biases influence financial decisions. This book aims to provide a comprehensive overview of these behavioural investment biases, their implications for investors and strategies for mitigating their impact.

Behavioural biases are systematic patterns of deviation from the norm or rationality in judgment, whereby inferences about other people and situations may be drawn in an illogical fashion. These biases can lead investors to make decisions that are not in their best financial interests. For example, confirmation bias leads individuals to favour information that confirms their preexisting beliefs or hypotheses, potentially ignoring contradictory evidence. This can result in an investor holding onto a losing stock based on selective information that supports their initial investment decision, rather than objectively assessing new information.

Another common bias is loss aversion, where the pain of losing is psychologically about twice as powerful as the pleasure of gaining. This can make investors overly cautious, leading them to miss out on lucrative opportunities. It can also lead to the disposition effect, where investors sell assets that have increased in value too early while holding onto assets that have decreased in value for too long.

This book will systematically explore these and other biases, including overconfidence, anchoring, herd behaviour and mental accounting, among others. Each chapter will focus on a specific bias, outlining its definition, demonstrating its effect on investment behaviour through real-world examples and empirical studies and providing practical advice on how to recognize and counteract these biases in one's own investment practice. Most importantly, we ask you – the reader – questions for self-reflection at the end of each section. When might you have been subject to one of these behavioural biases? What could you have done differently, and what might you do next time now that you are more aware of the bias?

To Be Biased Is to Be Human

Our aim is not to turn the investing population – or the general population for that matter – into robots without any emotion or behavioural quirks. On the contrary, we believe that your behavioural biases are, for the most part, a positive thing – they make you who you are. Your idiosyncrasies allow you to stand out from the crowd. They are why your friends like you, why you persevere, why you have hopes and dreams and why you will ultimately be so successful in life! But that doesn't mean we should not be aware of their presence in our everyday lives. Sometimes, checking our biases, leaving our quirks at the door and being 'less human' might lead us toward better outcomes.

To comprehend why humans exhibit behavioural investment biases, it's essential to look through the lens of evolution. Our ancestors faced a world fraught with immediate dangers and uncertainties, where quick decision-making often meant the difference between life and death. The cognitive mechanisms that evolved in response to these conditions are the precursors to today's behavioural biases.

These biases are not flaws per se but rather byproducts of an evolutionary process that favoured responsive, heuristic-based thinking over slower, more analytical thinking. In environments where speed was more valuable than accuracy, these biases served an adaptive purpose. However, while these mechanisms were once critical to our survival, in the modern world, especially in complex fields requiring careful deliberation and long-term planning like investing, they can misfire, leading to decisions that are not in our best interests.

While our target audience is investors – or the investor within each of you – the insights from behavioural finance have far-reaching implications, offering valuable lessons for improving decision-making in various domains and in everyday life. By understanding and addressing our biases, we can enhance our ability to make decisions that are not only financially sound but also wise and balanced in the broader context of our lives and society.

Whether you are a new investor looking to understand the psychological pitfalls that can affect your investment decisions or a seasoned professional seeking to refine your approach by incorporating insights from behavioural finance, we believe this book can offer valuable guidance. It is a resource for anyone interested in the intersection between psychology and finance and how understanding the former can lead to success in the latter.

PART 1

COGNITIVE BIASES

I. THE ANCHORING EFFECT

The Price Tag Trap

Maya adored the thrill of discovery at flea markets. Each trip was a treasure hunt for vintage finds, with the added spice of negotiation. On this sunny Saturday, a quaint side table caught her eye. Intricately carved with an air of antique elegance, it felt like a piece that had stories it yearned to tell.

As if anticipating her curiosity, the vendor introduced himself as Steve and launched into a sales pitch. 'This beauty is truly one-of-a-kind', he declared. 'Normally, I'd price it at $250, but for you, just today, $175 and it's all yours!'

Maya blinked. Her budget couldn't stretch to $250, but $175 sounded much more reasonable. Yet she hesitated. Was that still too much? The table did have some nicks and signs of age. Maybe Steve had intentionally thrown out a higher price at the start, knowing some back-and-forth bargaining would likely occur.

'I like it', Maya said carefully, testing the waters. 'Would you consider $150?'

Steve put on a show of exaggerated offence. 'Madam, your offer wounds me! $150 doesn't reflect the artistry, the timeless appeal...' His voice trailed off, as if pained by the low offer. After a carefully timed pause, he sighed: 'Tell you what, because it's you, $160 is the absolute lowest I can go.'

This back-and-forth had a familiar rhythm. Maya countered with $155, Steve feigned reluctance, and minutes later they shook hands on a $160 sale. As Maya carried her prize to the car, a wave of satisfaction washed over her. She had successfully bargained down the price – surely a mark of savvy deal-making.

Later, while dusting her 'new' piece, a question popped into Maya's head. What was the table truly worth? Should she have pressed for a deeper discount? Annoyed by this niggling doubt, she turned to online marketplaces. Her search results proved sobering. Similar tables, some arguably in better condition, were regularly selling for under $100.

Frustration settled in as Maya came to a stark realization: the vendor's initial $250 price wasn't a genuine appraisal. It was an anchor – a carefully chosen number to steer her away from the table's actual market value. The thrill of successful negotiation evaporated and was replaced by a lingering sense of having been misled.

The Anchoring Effect

The anchoring effect offers us insight into a fundamental aspect of human cognition with wide-reaching implications across various domains, notably in economic behaviour and financial decision-making. This cognitive bias illustrates how initial information sets a psychological benchmark that significantly influences subsequent judgments and decisions, often leading to systematic deviations from rationality.

The anchoring effect was first identified by psychologists Amos Tversky and Daniel Kahneman in the 1970s. They demonstrated that when individuals make estimates or decisions, they tend to start with an initially provided value (the anchor) and adjust from there to reach their conclusion. The critical insight was that the adjustments are typically insufficient, leaving the final judgment closer to the anchor than it would have been if the decision were made without such a reference point.

The anchoring effect operates through several mechanisms:

- **Insufficient Adjustment:** People make adjustments from the anchor to what they believe is the correct answer. However, these adjustments are often too small, partly because the initial anchor limits the range of possible outcomes considered.

- **Selective Accessibility:** The anchor makes certain information more accessible in our memory, leading us to overweight information that is consistent with the anchor and underweight contradictory information.

- **Priming:** Anchors can prime certain norms or expectations, subtly influencing how information is interpreted and what information is considered relevant.

Beyond the examples provided, the anchoring effect has profound implications in various fields:

- **Judicial Sentencing:** Initial sentencing recommendations can anchor judges' decisions, affecting the length of sentences given to defendants.

- **Financial Markets:** Analyst forecasts can serve as anchors, affecting investor expectations and market prices. Similarly, historical stock prices can anchor investors' expectations of future performance, influencing buying and selling decisions.

- **Consumer Behaviour:** Price tags, discounts and suggested donations can all serve as anchors, influencing how much consumers are willing to pay for goods or contribute to causes.

Understanding the anchoring effect allows for strategic exploitation, particularly in negotiations and marketing. Sellers can set high initial prices to anchor consumers' willingness to pay, while negotiators can use extreme initial offers to shift the zone of possible agreement in their favour.

To counteract the influence of anchoring, individuals should consider the following approaches:

- **Seek Out Multiple Perspectives:** Gathering diverse viewpoints can dilute the impact of a single anchor.

- **Establish Clear Criteria for Decision-Making:** Defining what information will guide your decisions in advance can reduce your susceptibility to irrelevant anchors.

- **Develop Awareness:** Simply being aware of the anchoring effect can help individuals adjust their decision-making processes to minimize its impact.

The anchoring effect underscores the bounded rationality of human decision-making, highlighting how judgments are not made in a vacuum but are deeply influenced by the context in which information is presented. By recognizing and understanding the mechanisms through which anchoring operates, individuals and organizations can devise strategies to mitigate its effects, leading to more informed and rational decision-making outcomes.

Questions for Self-Reflection

1. **Recalling Anchors:** Think about a recent purchase or negotiation. Can you identify any initial figures or claims that shaped your subsequent judgments?

2. **The Weight of First Impressions:** Consider situations where others presented you with facts or ideas before you could form your own opinion. Did those first impressions overly colour your perceptions?

3. **Countermeasures:** If you suspect an anchor is influencing your thinking, how can you challenge it? Could seeking independent estimates or alternative information be helpful?

4. **Using Anchors Positively:** The anchoring bias isn't always negative. Can you imagine how to use the 'power of first' positively, perhaps by setting an ambitious target in a goal-setting situation?

5. **Perspective Shifts:** Have you ever experienced a situation where you benefited from the anchoring effect? How does reflecting on that help you understand the subtle power of the anchor?

II. THE FUNDAMENTAL ATTRIBUTION ERROR

The Blame Game

Sarah slammed her laptop shut. Exhaustion, tinged with simmering rage, threatened to undo the carefully cultivated professional facade she'd spent years honing. Another impossible deadline barely met, another client placated and another round of 'motivational speeches' dished out to her seemingly disengaged team. She couldn't help feeling that her competence' was becoming a crutch for their inability to get things done.

Her mind flashed back to that morning's debacle. Jason – reliable and even-keeled Jason – had missed a key element in his code testing, which sent them all scrambling hours before a major demo. He'd looked genuinely startled when called out on it, mumbling something about a new system update interfering with his existing workflow. Sarah had barely controlled her snort of derision – just another mistake cloaked as an 'unexpected' technical issue. To her, it was increasingly clear Jason's work habits bordered on sabotage. There was a hidden undercurrent of resentment against her 'perfectionist' management style.

Then there was Monica, the design maestro with a complete disregard for schedules. When pressed, Monica would launch into long-winded lectures on 'the creative process' needing organic space to flow. It reeked of laziness to Sarah, especially when those artistic retreats routinely ended with a last-minute, caffeine-fuelled panic to finish what should have been completed days prior.

Her frustration felt like a constant background hum these days. She'd started noticing every minor error and misinterpreted email as further proof of a team stubbornly resistant to even basic professionalism. Each misstep, no matter how small, solidified her growing conviction that these weren't one-off hiccups; they were chronic behavioural problems ingrained in these individuals.

'Focus, Sarah, focus!' she hissed under her breath. There was still the matter of the quarterly review presentation. Numbers she herself had crunched into the early hours, only to find, just this morning, that the formatting Peter had promised her would need reworking. His cryptic email mentioning 'compatibility issues' with the design template held only the slightest hint of apology. This wasn't sloppiness anymore - not in Sarah's mind. This was open resistance masquerading as incompetence.

As she reread Peter's email, a flicker of doubt pricked her conscience'. It was true that their project management software did undergo one too many 'surprise' updates that seemed to constantly mess up existing integrations. But surely, by now, a seasoned pro like Peter should have found some workarounds and a way to compensate. Her inner monologue was cut short by a ping – another client demanding further changes to the scope of his project. She sighed. Perhaps this perpetual cycle of frustrations was an inevitable evil of management – having to drag entire teams, kicking and screaming, towards shared success.

The Fundamental Attribution Error

The fundamental attribution error (FAE), a cornerstone concept in social psychology, profoundly influences our understanding of human behaviour, particularly in interpreting others' actions. This cognitive bias leads us to overemphasize personality traits and underappreciate situational factors when explaining others' behaviours. Its implications are vast, stretching from interpersonal relationships to organizational dynamics and beyond.

The FAE was first described by psychologists Lee Ross and Edward E. Jones, who observed that people tend to attribute others' actions more to their character than to external circumstances. This bias occurs despite the fact that people recognize the role of situational factors in their own behaviour.

Several psychological mechanisms contribute to the FAE:

- **Actor-Observer Discrepancy:** As actors, we are acutely aware of the situational constraints we face; as observers, we lack a complete view of others' circumstances, leading us to default to dispositional explanations.

- **Cognitive Economy:** Attributing behaviour to stable personality traits simplifies the complex task of understanding human actions. It's cognitively easier to label someone as 'lazy' than to analyse the myriad situational factors that might influence their behaviour.

- **Cultural Influences:** Western cultures, which emphasize individualism, are particularly prone to the FAE. They foster a view of the self as independent and autonomous, leading to a greater focus on dispositional factors over situational ones.

The FAE can have significant implications across various domains:

- **Workplace Dynamics:** Misattributions can lead to misunderstandings and conflicts. For example, a manager might perceive an employee's missed deadline as a lack of commitment, overlooking situational factors like unclear instructions or resource constraints.

- **Legal and Judicial Systems:** The FAE can influence jury decisions, where jurors may attribute a defendant's actions more to character flaws than to situational pressures.

- **Interpersonal Relationships:** Misunderstandings fuelled by the FAE can strain relationships, as individuals may be quick to judge friends or partners without fully considering external stresses they may be experiencing.

Mitigating the FAE requires intentional effort to broaden one's perspective. Here are some strategies to consider:

- **Increase Situational Awareness:** Actively considering the external factors that might influence behaviour can counteract the tendency towards dispositional attributions.

- **Practice Perspective-Taking:** Imagining oneself in another's situation can help highlight the potential impact of situational factors.

- **Foster a Culture of Empathy:** In organizational contexts, promoting an understanding that behaviour is often a product of complex interactions between dispositional and situational factors can lead to more compassionate and effective responses to challenges.

- **Educate and Reflect:** Awareness and education about the FAE can prompt individuals to reflect on their attributions and adjust their judgments accordingly.

The fundamental attribution error underscores the complexity of human behaviour and the cognitive biases that shape our understanding of it. By recognizing and actively countering the FAE, we can foster more accurate, empathetic and constructive interpretations of others' actions, leading to improved interpersonal and organizational outcomes.

Questions for Self-Reflection

1. **Empathy vs Judgment:** When faced with a team member's failure, do you immediately focus on what they did wrong instead of the obstacles they could be facing?

2. **Self-Awareness in Error:** Do you find yourself assuming you would 'never make that mistake' without considering that you might be working with different information, skill sets and past experiences?

3. **Perceptions of Performance:** Have you formed judgments about how team members 'should' operate, and do you see a failure to fit your process as wilful insubordination or lack of skill?

4. **Approach to Feedback:** When giving feedback, do you use language that reflects blame ('You always…', 'You never…'), or do you try to frame it as an opportunity for joint problem-solving?

5. **Bias in Assessing Performance:** Does your own underperformance (or that of a favoured colleague) ever feel more justified due to 'uncontrollable' circumstances than when the same thing occurs to someone you view less favourably?

III. THE BACKFIRE EFFECT

When Facts Make Things Worse

Emily, with her unwavering commitment to public health, had always been a beacon of knowledge and advocacy within her community. Her passion for health and wellness wasn't just a personal interest; it was a call to action, a mission to inform and protect those around her. So, when a measles outbreak threatened her community, Emily saw it as her duty to step up and use her voice to combat the spread of the virus, as well as misinformation.

Armed with an array of evidence-based articles and the latest research findings, Emily took to social media, a platform she believed could amplify her message and educate her network on the critical importance of vaccinations. She crafted posts with care, ensuring they were both informative and accessible, and initiated discussions with friends and followers, presenting immunizations as the community's best defence against the outbreak.

Emily's intentions were pure, and her efforts were tireless. Yet, the response she received was not what she anticipated. Rather than fostering understanding and encouraging positive action, her posts became battlegrounds for debate. Counter-arguments flooded in, many citing long-discredited studies or leaning on anecdotal evidence, claiming vaccinations were dangerous. The more Emily tried to correct these misconceptions with facts, the more entrenched the opposition became.

The backlash was swift and disheartening. Emily watched in dismay as her attempts to educate and advocate seemed to only entrench anti-vaccination sentiment deeper within her circle. Friendships strained under the weight of heated exchanges, and Emily found herself at the centre of a storm of controversy she had never intended to create.

Confounded by the intensity of the resistance and the personal attacks that came with it, Emily began to question the efficacy of her approach. It was during this period of reflection that she encountered the concept of the backfire effect, a psychological phenomenon where presenting evidence that contradicts deeply held beliefs only serves to strengthen those beliefs. This understanding shed new light on her experience, offering an explanation for the counterintuitive intensification of anti-vaccination rhetoric in response to her efforts.

Realizing that her straightforward, fact-based approach might have been inadvertently reinforcing the very perspectives she sought to change, Emily embarked on a new strategy. She sought to understand the fears and concerns driving the anti-vaccination stance within her community, engaging in conversations with empathy and an open mind. By listening more and sharing personal stories that highlighted the positive impacts of vaccinations, Emily hoped to bridge the divide, fostering a dialogue based on mutual respect and understanding rather than confrontation.

This shift in approach marked a turning point. While not all were convinced, Emily's willingness to engage without judgment opened new avenues for discussion. She found that some were more receptive to reconsidering their stance.

Through her journey, Emily began to understand the complex dynamics of changing minds in an era of deeply entrenched beliefs. The backfire effect had taught her that the path to understanding and acceptance was not through confrontation but through compassionate dialogue and the sharing of human experiences. While the challenge was formidable, Emily remained committed to her mission, fortified by the belief that patience and empathy could, in time, bring about consensus and collective action for the health and wellbeing of her community.

The Backfire Effect

The backfire effect occurs when individuals presented with factual information contradicting their existing beliefs tend to double down on those very beliefs. The harder you try to dislodge the misconception, the more firmly it becomes rooted. While there are various types, here are some major ones to be aware of:

- **The Worldview Backfire Effect:** Core beliefs tied to identity are particularly resistant to challenge. Evidence contradicting deeply held moral, religious or political positions can trigger this phenomenon, as accepting that evidence would fundamentally redefine the person's understanding of themselves and the world.

- **The Familiarity Backfire Effect:** The very act of encountering a disproven myth strengthens the person's belief in it because it makes it feel familiar. Even explaining why something is incorrect requires repeating the misinformation, inadvertently causing it to seem more reliable.

- **The Overkill Backfire Effect:** Bombarding someone with too many counter-arguments, particularly in areas where emotions run high, can lead to further entrenchment. When people feel attacked, they're less receptive to logic.

Understanding the backfire effect opens a window into the psychology behind why facts often fail to persuade. Let's take a look at some of those psychological underpinnings:

- **Identity Protection:** For beliefs closely tied to personal identity, accepting contradictions poses a threat. Acknowledging they are wrong challenges our self-concept and the framework through which we understand the world.

- **Cognitive Dissonance:** When new information contradicts ingrained beliefs, we experience uncomfortable mental tension. Instead of revising our beliefs, it's easier to avoid, discredit or simply ignore the dissonance-causing evidence.

- **Tribal Mentality:** When group identification is strong, we prioritize conforming to group norms. Challenging widely held group beliefs can feel ostracizing, and so maintaining conformity often trumps a reasoned re-evaluation of our views.

The consequences of the backfire effect are significant in this era of widespread misinformation and societal polarization.

- **Erosion of Trust:** Repeated failed attempts to convince others with facts erodes trust between individuals' societal factions, and even in authority figures like scientists and journalists.

This breeds an environment where unsubstantiated rumours thrive.

- **Impeded Progress:** Societal initiatives, from science-based policy efforts to collective action addressing issues like climate change, are hindered when strong beliefs override sound evidence.

- **A Widening Divide:** In politics, and even within communities, the backfire effect reinforces the 'us vs them' mentality, where rational conversation and the search for common ground become harder to achieve.

The backfire effect doesn't mean it's impossible to change minds. It just means that the process becomes more nuanced, requiring empathy and communication tools that can address the deeper psychological needs driving those beliefs. Let's consider some strategies:

- **Common Ground First:** Seek areas of agreement before venturing into more difficult terrain. Establishing connection and a sense of shared values fosters trust and a foundation for more receptive exchanges.

- **Ask, Don't Tell:** Engage with curiosity rather than confrontation. Invite someone to explain how they formed their beliefs rather than trying to force your view on them. When people feel heard, defensiveness decreases.

- **Narrative Power:** Connect facts to relatable stories and lived experiences, weaving in shared emotions. Emotion often resonates more strongly than pure logic, especially when challenging values-based beliefs.

- **Affirmation Matters:** Instead of focusing solely on what's wrong, acknowledge valid aspects of a person's perspective, or affirm their right to hold different opinions. Respectful disagreement is more constructive than aggressive debate.

- **Plant Seeds, Not Trees:** Often, changing a deep-seated belief takes time. Consider subtly nudging people towards questioning their current stance by asking open-ended questions that stimulate their own critical thinking. A few insightful inquiries are more productive than an assault of facts.

- **Choose Your Battles:** Some beliefs are so ingrained that the effort to change them may be wasted. Recognizing when you're hitting a wall with someone will save your energy and maintain the relationship. Prioritize conversations where there is the possibility of open-mindedness.

- **Fact Check with Care:** Exposing false information is key, but how you do it matters. Debunk the myth head-on, but then emphasize solutions. Providing alternate, reliable sources fills the gap left by their old belief. This reduces cognitive dissonance.

IV. THE FRAMING EFFECT

The Slippery Slope of Wording

Mark found himself at a crossroads, faced with a decision. The choice seemed deceptively simple, yet it was fraught with complexity. His investment advisor, a seasoned professional known for his analytical acumen, had laid out two paths before him, each with its own promise of potential gains. The options were mirror images of each other in terms of expected returns, associated risks, and investment duration. Yet, Mark was ensnared in a web of indecision, unable to lean definitively towards one choice or the other.

The first option, presented with an air of optimism, was described as having a 70% chance of safeguarding his initial investment. It was a comforting thought, and the feeling of preservation and security appealed to Mark's cautious nature. The second option, however, was framed in starkly different terms – a 30% risk of losing a portion of his capital. Despite their logical equivalence, the two descriptions evoked vastly different emotional reactions in Mark. Where one whispered promises of safety, the other murmured warnings of peril.

Caught in the thrall of these conflicting emotions, Mark oscillated between the two choices, each shift in perspective bringing a fresh wave of doubt. The disparity in how the options were presented – though numerically identical – cast a shadow over his decision-making process, leaving him adrift in a sea of uncertainty.

In his quest for clarity, Mark turned to the vast expanse of investment wisdom at his fingertips, diving into financial journals, online forums and scholarly articles. It was during this journey that he encountered a concept that struck a chord deep within him: the framing effect. This cognitive bias, characterized by the influence of presentation over substance, explained his inertia.

Armed with this newfound understanding, Mark realized that his indecision was not a product of the options themselves but of the subtle yet powerful influence of their framing. The realization that he had been swayed by the manner in which the choices were presented, rather than their intrinsic merits, was both enlightening and liberating.

Mark revisited his options, this time with a critical eye, peeling away the layers of framing to reveal the core facts underneath. Freed from the emotional weight of the wording, he found himself able to evaluate with newfound objectivity.

This introspective journey led Mark to a deeper understanding of his own biases, the subtle forces that shape our choices and the complex interplay between perception and reality. By recognizing the framing effect at play, he not only navigated his way through this particular financial decision but also gained valuable insight into the mechanics of human judgment and the importance of vigilance in the face of cognitive biases.

In the end, Mark's decision was informed not by the seductive pull of language but by a balanced assessment of the facts, a testament to his growth as both an investor and a critical thinker. This experience, a confluence of challenge and discovery, left Mark with a richer appreciation for the intricacies of decision-making in the uncertain world of investment.

The Framing Effect

The framing effect is a cognitive bias that underscores the profound impact of context and presentation on our decision-making process. By altering how options are presented, framing can significantly influence our choices without altering the substantive content of the options themselves. This effect plays a critical role in fields ranging from marketing to politics as well as in our personal relationships and self-perception, demonstrating the power of language and context in shaping human behaviour.

The framing effect was extensively studied by psychologists Daniel Kahneman and Amos Tversky, who demonstrated that people react differently to a choice depending on whether it is presented in terms of potential losses or gains. This phenomenon is rooted in prospect theory, which posits that people value gains and losses differently, leading to inconsistent decision-making when the same choice is framed in different ways.

Several psychological mechanisms contribute to the framing effect:

- **Risk Aversion and Loss Aversion:** People tend to be risk-averse when a choice is framed positively but risk-seeking when a choice is framed negatively. This is closely related to loss aversion, where losses are felt more acutely than gains.

- **Cognitive Bias:** The framing effect illustrates how individuals rely on cognitive shortcuts (heuristics) to make decisions, with the frame serving as a shortcut that influences the perceived attractiveness of options.

- **Emotional Influence:** Emotional reactions to different framings can significantly influence decision-making, with positive frames eliciting positive emotions and negative frames often triggering fear or aversion.

The framing effect has wide-reaching implications:

- **Healthcare Decisions:** The way health interventions are framed can significantly affect patient choices, such as choosing between treatments based on survival rates versus mortality rates.

- **Financial Behaviour:** Investment choices, savings plans and retirement options are all susceptible to framing, with the presentation of risk and reward influencing financial decisions.

- **Environmental Policy:** Public support for environmental policies can be shaped by framing these policies in terms of the benefits of action (gain frame) versus the costs of inaction (loss frame).

- **Legal and Ethical Decision-Making:** Legal judgments and ethical decisions can be swayed by how scenarios are framed, affecting perceptions of guilt, responsibility and justice.

To counteract the influence of framing, individuals should consider the following strategies:

- **Critical Thinking:** It's important to develop the habit of critically evaluating how information is presented, questioning the frame and considering the information from multiple perspectives.

- **Awareness and Education:** Becoming aware of framing and its effects can help individuals recognize when their decision-making might be influenced by the presentation rather than the substance of the options.

- **Seeking Neutral Information:** Looking for or requesting information presented in a neutral, unframed manner can aid in making more objective decisions.

The framing effect highlights the subtle yet powerful ways in which language and presentation can shape our perceptions, judgments and decisions. By understanding and recognizing this cognitive bias, individuals can become more adept at navigating the complex landscape of choices they face and making decisions that are more consistent with their values and objectives.

Questions for Self-Reflection

1. **Uncovering Your Weak Spots:** Can you identify areas in your life where you are particularly susceptible to the framing effect? Is it in your financial decisions, health choices or relationships? Recognizing those vulnerable areas gives you a focus to look out for framing manipulation.

2. **Analysing Your Emotional Trigger Points:** What kinds of word choices trigger strong emotional responses for you? Do terms like 'failure', 'sacrifice' or 'risk cause a disproportionate

reaction, making you less likely to weigh information rationally?

3. **Challenging the Frame:** Do you find yourself drawn to messages that promise gains? The next time you're confronted with a persuasive statement, question whether you would feel the same if the phrasing focused on the flipside – potential losses rather than gains.

4. **Seeking Alternate Frames:** When feeling swayed by a message, can you consciously practice framing it in an alternative way? For example, is a situation framed in a way that makes you feel anxious or fearful? Could you intentionally recast it to focus on opportunity or learning?

5. **Dissecting Persuasion:** In your interactions with others, can you spot where they might be leveraging the framing effect to nudge you towards a specific perspective or action? This includes politicians, salespeople and even friends and family who may be unconsciously using this technique.

V. APOPHENIA

The Market's Hidden Messages

In the intricate world of financial analysis, Alexander stood out as a maverick and a visionary whose unconventional methods and keen eye for patterns set him apart from his peers. He approached the stock market not merely as a series of numbers and trends but as a grand, cryptic narrative, each movement a clue to be deciphered, each fluctuation a whisper of what was to come. To Alexander, the market was a vast, interconnected web, with each thread revealing the potential for future shifts and hidden opportunities waiting to be uncovered by those patient and insightful enough to look beneath the surface.

His days were consumed with the analysis of market data as he delved deep into the labyrinth of financial reports, stock movements and economic indicators. With a meticulous hand, he crafted intricate charts and graphs, each a masterpiece of complexity that, to the untrained eye, appeared as bewildering as an abstract painting. Yet, to Alexander, these charts were clear maps to hidden treasures – guiding lights through the fog of market uncertainty.

One fateful day, Alexander stepped into his firm's investment committee meeting armed with his latest discovery – a series of correlations between seemingly disparate market indicators that, to him, spelled out an undeniable impending economic shift. With the fervour of a prophet, he laid out his findings for his colleagues, his voice steady, his conviction unwavering. He drew parallels with past market events, citing instances where similar patterns had foreshadowed significant changes, painting a compelling picture of the opportunity that lay before them.

Despite their scepticism, Alexander's passion and the depth of his analysis could not be easily dismissed by the investment committee. Accustomed to more traditional approaches, they nevertheless found themselves caught in the gravitational pull of Alexander's certainty. Though doubts lingered, the sheer force of his belief and the allure of his predictions prompted them to entertain the possibility he presented. In a move that was as much a testament to their trust in Alexander's acumen as it was a hedge against the unknown, they decided to make minor adjustments to their investment strategy, a nod to the potential he had laid before them.

As the months unfolded, the anticipation of the predicted economic shift grew. Alexander watched the market with the intensity of a hawk, ready to see his predictions come to fruition. Yet, as time passed, the seismic shift he had foreseen failed to materialize. The patterns he had identified did not culminate in the dramatic events he had anticipated. The market, in its unfathomable complexity, continued on its path, seemingly indifferent to the clear signals Alexander had observed.

This realization was a humbling one for Alexander. It served as a poignant reminder of the inherent unpredictability of financial markets, a system influenced by a myriad of factors, many beyond the grasp of any one analyst, no matter how insightful. And it underscored the danger of overreliance on pattern recognition in a realm where chaos and order dance in endless interplay, where for every pattern that predicts the future, countless others lead nowhere.

In the aftermath, Alexander's journey became a valuable case study within his firm – a lesson on the limits of data interpretation. It highlighted the importance of balancing innovative analysis with the humility to acknowledge the market's capacity for randomness; the need for caution to temper conviction. For Alexander, it was a moment of introspection'. Though his predictions had not come to pass, his quest for understanding continued, driven by the belief that within the market's chaos lays the potential for insight, if only one knows where to look.

Apophenia

Apophenia is the human tendency to perceive meaningful patterns within random data. The term, coined by psychiatrist Klaus Conrad, describes a cognitive bias that leads individuals to mistakenly attribute significance to the coincidental occurrence of events.

Apophenia stems from the brain's pattern-detection mechanisms, which are essential for survival. Recognizing patterns allows us to predict and interpret complex phenomena. However, this same mechanism can lead us astray, especially when we attempt to find order in randomness, as our brains are predisposed to seek out meaning, even when none exists.

In the context of investing, apophenia can manifest in various ways:

- **Overinterpreting Market Indicators:** Investors may believe they see patterns in stock prices, economic indicators or global events that seem to predict future market behaviour.

- **Conspiracy Theories:** In extreme cases, apophenia can lead to conspiracy thinking, where investors believe that certain events must be connected in meaningful ways, despite a lack of evidence.

To counteract apophenia, investors can use the following strategies:

- **Statistical Testing:** Use statistical methods to test the validity of perceived patterns.

- **Seeking Second Opinions:** Consult with colleagues or use advisory services to get an objective take on market data.

- **Longitudinal Analysis:** Look at long-term trends and data to distinguish between actual patterns and random occurrences.

Questions for Self-Reflection

1. **Pattern Recognition vs Coincidence:** Have you ever acted on a perceived pattern in market data that turned out to be a coincidence? What was the outcome?

2. **Trend Analysis:** How do you differentiate between meaningful market trends and random noise when analysing data?

3. **Decision-Making:** Reflect on a time when you might have experienced apophenia. How did it affect your decision-making process, and how can you guard against it in the future?

4. **Evidence-Based Investing:** What systems do you have in place to ensure that your investment decisions are based on robust evidence rather than perceived patterns?

5. **Balancing Openness and Scepticism:** How do you maintain a balance between being open to new interpretations of market data and avoiding the trap of seeing connections where none exist?

VI. THE ILLUSION OF CONTROL

Rituals of Chance

David, an astute financial analyst with a deep-rooted passion for poker, had honed his analytical prowess over years of meticulous work and strategic gameplay. His days were consumed with dissecting market trends and financial reports, while his evenings were often spent around the poker table, engaging in a battle of wits and patience. David's success in both arenas wasn't just a testament to his skills but also to his unique blend of logic and personal rituals. He harboured a profound belief in his ability to sway outcomes in his favour, which was bolstered by a series of routines and superstitions that he followed religiously. Whether it was wearing his lucky shirt to a poker game or analysing financial markets at a specific time of day, David's rituals were an integral part of his strategy for success.

At work, David's knack for making lucrative stock picks had earned him the respect of his peers and a reputation as a rising star in the financial world. His decisions were not only based on thorough analysis but also on gut feelings that he attributed to his understanding of the market's ebb and flow – a sense that he likened to reading a poker opponent's body language to determine their next move. In poker, his ability to call someone's bluff and take calculated risks had made him a formidable player in high-stakes games, where he was known for his cool demeanour and unwavering confidence.

However, one fateful evening, David's confidence was put to the test in a way it had never been before. Seated at a table with seasoned players, the stakes were higher than usual, and the atmosphere was charged with tension. As the game progressed, David found himself in an uncharacteristic losing streak. Each hand seemed to slip through his fingers, no matter how strategically he played or how closely he followed his rituals.

Yet, instead of exercising caution, each loss only fuelled his belief in his ability to turn things around. David's past successes, both in finance and poker, had cemented a sense of his own invincibility. He clung to the notion that his next move, a perfect blend of skill, analysis and superstition, would reverse his fortunes. It was this conviction that led him to make increasingly bold and risky bets, each time telling himself that control over the game's outcome was within his grasp.

As the night wore on, David's situation grew more precarious. His stack of chips dwindled, and the glances from his opponents grew more pitying and less wary. Yet, in his mind, the next hand always held the promise of redemption, of a return to the winning streak he was so accustomed to. This belief in his ability to defy the odds and influence the randomness of poker had always been his strength, but now it seemed to blind him to the reality of his situation.

In the world of high stakes and higher risks, David was learning a harsh lesson about the limits of control. Despite his analytical skills and rituals, the inherent uncertainty of poker was proving to be a formidable opponent. As the night reached its climax, David was faced with a decision. His next move could either lead to a miraculous comeback or seal his fate as a cautionary tale of overconfidence and the dangers of relying too heavily on superstition in the face of unfavourable odds.

The Illusion of Control

The illusion of control is a cognitive bias that leads individuals to overestimate their ability to control events and outcomes that are largely or entirely random. This bias can affect various aspects of our lives and decision-making, particularly in areas like gambling, financial investments and personal achievements.

The illusion of control was first identified by psychologist Ellen Langer in the 1970s. Langer's experiments demonstrated that people tend to believe their personal involvement or actions can influence the outcome of chance events, especially when those events have features typically associated with skill-based activities.

Several factors contribute to the illusion of control:

- **Familiarity:** Engaging frequently in an activity can create a false sense of expertise and control over its outcome.

- **Choice:** Having the ability to choose or influence decisions in a situation can lead to an exaggerated belief in one's control over the result.

- **Personal Involvement:** Active participation in processes, even in a minimal or symbolic way, can enhance our sense of control.

- **Previous Success:** Past successes, especially if attributed to personal skill or strategy, can reinforce the belief in one's ability to influence future outcomes.

In financial markets, the illusion of control can lead investors to overestimate their ability to predict and influence market movements, resulting in overtrading, under-diversification and increased risk-taking. This bias can also affect perceptions of risk, with individuals underestimating the probability of negative outcomes for actions they believe they control.

To mitigate the illusion of control in financial decision-making, individuals should consider the following strategies:

- **Seek Diverse Perspectives:** Consulting with others can provide alternative viewpoints and challenge one's assumptions.

- **Adopt a Long-Term Perspective:** Focusing on long-term investment strategies can reduce the temptation to overestimate control over short-term market fluctuations.

- **Embrace Probabilistic Thinking:** Recognizing the inherent randomness in markets and focusing on probabilities rather than certainties can help align strategies with reality.

Questions for Self-Reflection

1. **The Illusion of Control in Random Outcomes:** Have you ever overestimated your influence over a situation with a random

outcome, like a stock investment or a game of chance? Reflect on what led you to feel in control.

2. **Hindsight Analysis of Control:** Consider a decision where you believed you had control over the outcome. In hindsight, what factors were out of your control, and how did they impact the result?

3. **Familiarity Bias and Outcome Control:** Think about a time when familiarity with a task led you to overestimate your ability to control its outcome. How can recognizing this bias change your approach to similar situations in the future?

4. **Perceived Control and Decision-Making:** Reflect on how your personal involvement in a process or your ability to make choices about it influenced your perception of control. Were there instances where this led to suboptimal decisions?

5. **Risk Perception and Control:** Evaluate how your perception of risk changes in situations where you feel a sense of control. How can understanding the illusion of control help you make more informed risk assessments?

VII. PROPORTIONALITY BIAS

The Magnitude Misconception

Isaac Thompson had long been the go-to equity analyst for deep dives into company fundamentals, earning acclaim for his meticulous dissections of balance sheets, cash flow statements and growth prospects. His analytical prowess was grounded in a philosophy that significant shifts in a company's stock price were invariably the result of equally significant developments within or around the company. This belief system had served him well throughout his career, guiding his investment recommendations and strategy formulations with considerable success.

However, the financial landscape, ever-evolving under the influence of technology and new media, was about to offer Isaac a challenging lesson on its unpredictability. The unexpected catalyst came in the form of a relatively obscure tech startup, whose stock price experienced an abrupt and astronomical rise. This surge seemed utterly disconnected from the company's current market standing or any recent achievements of note – a puzzle that caught Isaac's attention and defied his fundamental approach to analysis.

While Isaac's peers quickly pointed to a viral phenomenon as the cause – a social media post from a well-known influencer that had unexpectedly catapulted the startup into the spotlight – Isaac found this explanation difficult to accept. To him, the idea that a mere post, irrespective of its viral reach, could so dramatically influence a company's valuation undermined the market principles he held dear.

Convinced that there must be a more substantial reason lurking beneath the surface, Isaac embarked on an exhaustive investigation.

He sifted through recent news releases for any mention of a major merger or acquisition, combed through patent databases for evidence of a groundbreaking new technology and scrutinized the startup's financial statements for hidden clues that might explain their stock's sudden ascent. Isaac was driven by the conviction that the market's movements, however erratic they appeared, were ultimately rational and grounded in material events.

Yet, as the days passed and the stock gradually returned to its pre-spike levels, it became increasingly clear that Isaac's search was yielding nothing. There were no secret mergers, no revolutionary patents awaiting approval and no undisclosed financial windfalls. The surge, it seemed, was exactly what his peers had suggested – a flash in the pan driven by the influence of a singular online personality and the ephemeral whims of social media users.

This realization was a bitter pill for Isaac to swallow as it challenged his fundamental beliefs. It was a stark introduction to the realities of the market landscape in the digital age, where traditional metrics of value and performance driven by tangible events can be momentarily, yet profoundly, overshadowed by the seemingly trivial yet powerful forces of social media.

For Isaac, this was more than just a missed call on a stock movement; it was a lesson in humility and adaptability. It underscored the need to broaden his analytical lens to include the increasingly significant role that social media and public sentiment play in the valuation of companies, especially those in the tech sector, where investor perceptions can be as volatile as the technology is disruptive.

He recognized that traditional analyses and conventional financial models must now contend with the rapid spread of information – and misinformation – across global networks. In this context, he had to remain open to new variables and indicators – a reminder that in the fluid and fast-paced world of stock trading, sometimes the smallest spark can ignite the most significant changes.

Proportionality Bias

The proportionality bias is the inclination to assume that big events have big causes, correlating the size or impact of an outcome with the significance of its cause. This bias leads people to expect that significant events – like major stock market moves, political upheavals or historical milestones – must be the result of equally substantial and deliberate causes.

This bias originates from the human tendency to seek meaningful explanations that match the scale of an event. It's a form of cognitive dissonance as the idea of small causes leading to significant effects can seem incongruous, so the mind searches for a more fitting explanation. This bias is related to our innate need for understanding and control, where more obvious explanations provide a sense of predictability and order.

In the financial world, the proportionality bias can cause analysts and investors like Isaac to overlook or dismiss the actual drivers of market movements, particularly in an age where information and influence are decentralized. In the modern market, small-scale events can indeed precipitate large-scale reactions, often due to the interconnectedness and speed of information dissemination.

Investors can combat this bias by using these strategies:

- **Recognize Influence Dynamics:** We can change our perception simply by understanding that in today's digital world small causes can have large effects due to the rapid spread of information.

- **Focus on Probabilities:** Evaluate market events based on statistical probabilities rather than perceived significance.

- **Maintain Flexibility:** Be prepared to accept that the market's reaction to events can be disproportionate and adjust your strategies accordingly.

Questions for Self-Reflection

1. **Oversimplification of Market Events:** Can you recall a time when you attributed a major market event to a cause without considering the possibility of smaller, less obvious influences?

2. **Evaluating News Impact on Investments:** How do you assess the potential impact of news or events on your investments? Do you account for the disproportionate influence that social media and rapid communication can have?

3. **Proportionality Bias and Missed Opportunities:** Reflect on a situation where believing in proportionality bias might have

led you to miss an investment opportunity or misjudge a risk. How could you have approached your analysis differently?

4. **Safeguarding Against Proportionality Bias in Strategy:** Consider how the proportionality bias might affect your long-term investment strategy. Are there safeguards you can put in place to prevent missed insights due to this bias?

5. **Evidence-Based Cause and Effect Analysis:** What strategies can you adopt to ensure that you are evaluating causes and effects in the market based on evidence and probabilities rather than the expected size of their impact?

VIII. THE NARRATIVE FALLACY

The Story Behind the Numbers

Sophia, with her sterling reputation as an investment analyst, had always navigated the complexities of market data, industry reports and economic indicators with unparalleled precision. Her knack for dissecting intricate financial information and her foresight in predicting market trends had not only bolstered her career but had also made her insights highly sought after in her firm. Renowned for her analytical prowess, Sophia approached each project with a rigorous methodology.

However, Sophia's latest assignment plunged her into uncharted waters. Tasked with scrutinizing a nascent industry characterized by its buzz and rapidly evolving landscape, she found herself at the crossroads of innovation and speculation. This sector, buoyed by technological advances and shifting consumer preferences, was in a state of flux, presenting a challenge to Sophia's reliance on quantitative data. The industry's dynamic nature, coupled with the hype surrounding it, made traditional analysis methods less reliable, necessitating a more nuanced approach.

Struggling to unravel the complexities of this burgeoning industry, Sophia crafted a narrative, rich in optimism and underscored by data and trends from both media stories and industry forecasts, painting a vivid picture of a sector on the brink of exponential success and profitability. She delved into the drivers of this potential expansion: technological breakthroughs promising to revolutionize the market, evolving consumer behaviours that aligned with the industry's offerings and anticipated regulatory changes poised to facilitate its growth. Sophia's report, reflective of the prevailing enthusiasm, resonated with the bullish outlook of investors and industry observers alike, projecting an image of inevitable prosperity for companies within the sector.

As time went by, however, the foundational pillars of Sophia's analysis began to show cracks. The technological innovations that were expected to catapult the industry forward encountered significant obstacles, revealing complexities and challenges that were initially underestimated. Consumer adoption, critical for the industry's success, progressed at a pace far slower than anticipated. Regulatory developments veered off the anticipated path too, introducing new hurdles rather than removing existing ones. The expectation of rapid growth and widespread adoption began to wane as the reality of the' situation became increasingly apparent.

This stark divergence from Sophia's optimistic projections served as a sobering reminder of the market's unpredictability. Her 'narrative now appeared to be an oversimplification of an inherently complex and uncertain industry. It highlighted the limitations of predictive narratives in the face of an ever-changing market landscape, underscoring the necessity of tempering optimism with a careful consideration of potential challenges and obstacles.

For Sophia, this project became a pivotal learning experience. It illuminated the critical importance of flexibility in analysis, the need to continuously update assumptions with emerging data and the value of incorporating a range of scenarios, including less optimistic outcomes. It also prompted Sophia to refine her analytical approach, embracing a more balanced perspective that accounted for both the potential for success and the risks of setbacks. This shift not only enhanced the depth and resilience of her future analyses but also reinforced the principle that in the realm of investment a growth narrative must always be weighed against the realities of an unpredictable and rapidly changing market.

The Narrative Fallacy

The narrative fallacy is a cognitive bias that compels individuals to weave coherent stories out of scattered or unrelated facts, particularly when interpreting past events or predicting future outcomes. This bias towards storytelling over statistical and empirical evidence can significantly impact our decision-making process, especially in complex fields like investing, where the allure of a compelling narrative can overshadow the cold, hard data.

The narrative fallacy arises from several key aspects of human psychology:

- **Cognitive Ease:** Our brains prefer simplicity and are inclined towards information that is easily processed and understood. A coherent story is much more palatable than complex, disjointed data.

- **Memory and Recall:** Humans are more likely to remember information that is presented as a story. Narratives have a structure that makes them memorable, facilitating recall.

- **Pattern Recognition:** Humans have evolved to recognize patterns as a survival mechanism. This ability, while beneficial, can lead us to falsely perceive patterns and causality where none exist, forming the basis of narrative construction.

- **Need for Meaning:** People have an inherent need to find meaning in their experiences. Narratives fulfil this need by providing a sense of understanding and control over events and information.

The narrative fallacy has some related concepts:

- **Confirmation Bias:** This is the tendency to search for, interpret, favour and recall information in a way that confirms one's preexisting beliefs or hypotheses. This can lead us to selectively use data that fits a narrative while ignoring contradictory evidence.

- **Representativeness Heuristic:** This is a mental shortcut that involves making judgments about the probability of an uncertain event, which can lead to overestimating the likeliness of simplistic stories.

- **The Availability Heuristic:** This is the tendency to overestimate the importance of information that is available or easily recalled, which often pertains to narrative elements.

In the world of investing, the narrative fallacy can lead to several detrimental outcomes:

- **Overconfidence in Predictions:** Investors may become overly confident in their predictions about market movements or the success of certain investments based on compelling stories, leading to risky decisions.

- **Missed Opportunities:** A strong narrative can cause investors to overlook solid opportunities that don't fit into a compelling story or to ignore emerging risks that are not part of the narrative.

- **Herd Behaviour:** When a particular narrative gains traction, it can lead to herd behaviour, with investors collectively moving in a direction that might not be supported by objective facts.

- **Market Volatility:** The widespread adoption of certain narratives can contribute to increased market volatility, as investments are made and withdrawn based on the strength of the story rather than economic indicators.

To counteract the narrative fallacy, individuals and organizations can adopt several strategies:

- **Diverse Information Sources:** Actively seeking information from a variety of sources can help challenge the dominance of a single narrative.

- **Critical Thinking:** Developing critical thinking skills, including questioning assumptions and seeking evidence, can help evaluate the validity of narratives.

- **Structured Analytical Techniques:** Employing structured analytical techniques, such as scenario analysis, can help us to assess our predictions without relying solely on narrative coherence.

- **Emphasis on Empirical Evidence:** Prioritizing empirical evidence and statistical analysis over storytelling in our decision-making process can reduce the impact of the narrative fallacy.

Questions for Self-Reflection

1. **Story vs Data:** Can you recall an investment decision you made that was more heavily influenced by a compelling story than by comprehensive data analysis? What was the outcome?

2. **Guarding Against the Narrative Fallacy:** How do you ensure you're not succumbing to the narrative fallacy when evaluating potential investments, especially in sectors surrounded by hype?

3. **Challenging the Investment Narrative:** Reflect on a time when disconfirming evidence challenged your investment narrative. How did you respond, and what did you learn from the experience?

4. **Probabilistic Thinking:** In what ways can you incorporate probabilistic thinking into your investment analysis to counteract the allure of simple narratives?

5. **Promoting Critical Thinking in Teams:** How can you foster a culture within your team or organization that values diverse perspectives and critical thinking to guard against the narrative fallacy?

IX. THE GAMBLER'S FALLACY

Chasing the Elusive Pattern

The gambling hall held a unique intensity tonight, a far cry from Mark's usual realm of meticulous spreadsheets and long-term valuation models. It was a planned detour, a foray into Vegas during a business trip, mostly for light-hearted observation; a chance to peek behind the curtain at a world seemingly driven more by adrenaline than algorithms. Yet, here he was, hours later, immersed at the roulette table, his sense of controlled detachment unravelling with each spin of the wheel.

Initially, it wasn't the lure of immediate winnings that encouraged him to play but a purely analytical curiosity. Red had dominated with alarming consistency. Nine, 10, then an impossible 12 reds in a row! In theory, Mark knew every spin was an independent event with roughly 50/50 odds (aside from the slight edge the casino always had). His fund specialized in quantitative methods, emphasizing mathematical probabilities over hunches and hot streaks. However, there was a seductive dissonance playing out inside him. One part of his mind screamed about statistical anomalies, outliers within large datasets, with an eventual reversion to the mean. The other voice whispered of hidden codes and the tantalizing, albeit irrational, thrill of deciphering a streak on the brink of breaking. Clearly, a black *must* be due, after so many reds in a row.

This wasn't a sudden descent into reckless gambling. He meticulously charted each result, searching for the turning point – not out of blind belief but a gnawing uncertainty. Could such a consistent streak be simply the workings of pure chance? Was he succumbing to the same intoxicating illusion that fuels desperate players betting their rent money in backroom games? His analytical training demanded proof – hard evidence to counter the gambler's instinct.

With each black hit after those long reds, the illusion took hold once again. See, there it was! A sense of vindication and the thrill of an anticipated shift. But it was quickly squashed by the next spin revealing yet another red. In his mind, a battle unfolded – the trained analyst wrestling with a growing desire to trust a seemingly impossible pattern.

A deep breath and a glance at his watch jolted Mark out of his trance. This wasn't a mathematical puzzle with elegant solutions. The casino's atmosphere pulsated with an energy designed to exploit the very instincts warring within him. Tonight, rational thought felt strangely fragile.

Stepping back from the table, Mark observed another player double their bet after a win, their face mirroring his own prior excitement. It was a stark reminder of the vortex he was almost sucked into. He left the casino floor not with winnings or losses but a troubling yet visceral reminder of how easily the mind could be deceived. There was comfort in the cold probabilities of his usual world of finance. His Vegas detour wasn't a failure, but a powerful, personal lesson about the dangers of seeking order within pure randomness.

The Gambler's Fallacy

The gambler's fallacy, also known as the Monte Carlo fallacy or the fallacy of the maturity of chances, is a cognitive bias that significantly impacts decision-making in scenarios involving randomness. This fallacy is particularly prevalent in gambling, investing and in situations where individuals interpret sequences of independent events. It stems from the erroneous belief that if a particular outcome occurs more frequently than normal during a past period, it will happen less frequently in the future, or vice versa.

One of the core aspects of the gambler's fallacy is a fundamental misunderstanding of probability. In situations where events are independent – meaning the outcome of one event does not influence the outcome of another – the likelihood of a specific outcome remains constant. For instance, the probability of flipping a coin and landing on heads is always 50%, regardless of how many times heads has come up in previous flips. However, our brains struggle to internalize this concept, leading us to believe that previous outcomes can somehow influence future results.

The gambler's fallacy is often compounded by the illusion of control, a bias that makes individuals overestimate their ability to control or influence outcomes. In scenarios where people can make choices, such as selecting lottery numbers or deciding on which colour to bet in roulette, they often feel a sense of agency that is disconnected from the reality of the situation. This perceived control can lead individuals to make decisions based on the mistaken belief that they can predict or sway random outcomes.

Another factor contributing to the gambler's fallacy is the representativeness heuristic, a mental shortcut that leads us to judge the likelihood of an event by how closely it matches our expectations of a model or sequence. We expect sequences of random events to appear representative of what we perceive as 'randomness', meaning they include a balance of different outcomes. For example, after witnessing several instances of red on a roulette wheel, we might incorrectly assume that black is 'due' to occur, as we expect the outcomes to balance out.

The clustering illusion also has a part to play in this. It refers to our tendency to see patterns in random sequences. Our brains are wired to find order in chaos, leading us to erroneously identify streaks or clusters in data as significant when they are merely the product of random variation. This illusion can cause individuals to interpret random sequences in the stock market or while gambling, for instance, as having predictive value, leading to misguided decisions based on trends that do not exist.

In the realm of investing, the gambler's fallacy can lead to several detrimental behaviours. Investors might avoid or sell stocks that have experienced a series of gains, believing them to be 'due' for a loss, or conversely, they may invest in stocks that have been declining under the mistaken belief that a turnaround is imminent. Such decisions, based on the expectation that past trends will eventually reverse, can result in poorly timed trades and missed opportunities. Additionally, the fallacy can lead to overtrading, as investors chase perceived patterns that are not grounded in sound investment analysis or strategy.

Understanding the gambler's fallacy and recognizing its influence on decision-making is crucial for anyone engaged in activities involving randomness and risk. By acknowledging the independence of events and resisting the urge to find patterns in randomness, individuals can make more rational decisions, whether in gambling, investing or everyday life.

Questions for Self-Reflection

1. **Recognizing the Seduction of Patterns:** When have you felt strongly drawn to a pattern or trend, even when the evidence didn't fully support it? What fuelled that feeling?

2. **Gut Instinct vs Data:** Have you faced situations where your intuition urged you in one direction, but data or logic seemed to suggest the opposite? How did you resolve that conflict?

3. **The Illusion of Control:** In what areas of your life do you struggle to recognize the difference between things you can control and those influenced by chance or circumstances you have no influence over?

4. **Moments of Self-Deception:** Can you think of a time when you convinced yourself of something in order to justify a decision or belief, even if it went against available information?

5. **Learning from Mistakes:** In retrospect, what would you have done differently in a situation where you were drawn in by a deceptive pattern or misleading gut feeling?

X. OVERCONFIDENCE BIAS

When Conviction Outpaces Reality

Alex had climbed the ladder of the investment world with impressive speed. Armed with a reputable MBA and fuelled by early successful trades, he developed a reputation for decisive action and a strong conviction behind his investment choices. Colleagues at the mid-sized wealth management firm where he worked frequently sought his opinion on market trends and the viability of specific investment vehicles. For the most part, his instincts had served him well.

Now, an opportunity arose that ignited his excitement. A young tech startup specializing in blockchain-based asset management pitched Alex and several other potential investors. Their audacious proposal promised to revolutionize secure transactions and disrupt traditional asset tracking. While not deeply experienced in the specifics of blockchain technology, Alex recognized a potentially massive untapped market. The charismatic founding team exuded confidence.

The pitch deck included rosy financial projections, but on closer examination, the growth rates and user adoption timelines seemed overly optimistic. Several of Alex's colleagues expressed reservations, noting that the regulatory environment for the space was still developing and highlighting the high failure rate of early-stage tech ventures.

Alex, however, found himself increasingly drawn to the potential windfall. Something about the founders' passionate vision resonated with his natural penchant for bold action. After all, some of his greatest career successes sprang from investing early in companies that established industry players had mistakenly dismissed. This, he decided, felt like a similar contrarian opportunity.

With his typical self-assured demeanour, Alex advocated strongly for investing in the blockchain startup. While initial investment from the firm was cautious, others began to be swayed by his persuasiveness and seeming ability to spot hidden gems before competitors caught on. Alex increased his personal investment, leveraging connections to bring additional funding to the venture.

Yet, within the first year, problems surfaced. Adoption by institutional investors was slower than anticipated, security concerns in a separate but related cryptocurrency case made headlines, shaking public confidence in blockchain as a whole, and infighting within the startup's leadership caused key talent to leave. Alex's once-firm conviction wavered. Had he succumbed to his own hype? Were his earlier dismissals of colleagues' concerns born less of true insight and more of his stubborn ego and unwillingness to consider counter-arguments?

In the second year, the firm decided to sell its stake in the venture at a significant loss. Several clients withdrew investments from Alex's management following the debacle, tarnishing his reputation as a rising star within the organization. This painful experience became a turning point in his career.

Overconfidence Bias

Alex's experience starkly demonstrates the harmful impact of overconfidence bias, a phenomenon that is especially prevalent in high-stakes industries like finance. Overconfidence bias encompasses several interconnected behavioural tendencies:

- **The Illusion of Control:** Overconfident individuals overestimate their ability to predict and control outcomes, leading to excessive risk-taking. They view events as subject to their skill rather than acknowledging the element of chance or uncontrollable factors.

- **The Above-Average Effect:** We tend to have an inflated view of our own capabilities relative to others. This fosters belief in our superior analytical prowess or access to unique knowledge, making us less receptive to alternative views.

- **Hindsight Bias:** After positive outcomes, we become prone to 'I knew it all along' distortions, rewriting our thought processes to create a sense of inevitability about past success. This reinforces the notion of personal invincibility.

- **Attribution Bias:** We often attribute successes to our own skill while framing setbacks as bad luck or driven by external factors. This creates a feedback loop which only strengthens the overconfidence cycle.

Overconfidence in investing can lead to the following problems:

- **Underestimating Risk:** Ignoring past market data or downplaying volatility becomes common when a sense of infallibility takes hold.

- **Under-Diversification:** Excessive belief in specific trades leads to underestimating the importance of diverse portfolios for managing risk.

- **Neglecting Due Diligence:** Intuition may sometimes be helpful, but overconfident individuals undervalue meticulous research and external viewpoints.

Questions for Self-Reflection

1. **Challenging Past Performance:** Is your assessment of your own skills based mostly on successful trades? Are you ignoring your failures and what they can teach you?

2. **Contrarian Stance:** Do you pride yourself on identifying trends early? How do you distinguish that from blindly going against mainstream advice?

3. **Devil's Advocate:** Can you create systems for consistently seeking contrary views and actively testing your own investment theses?

4. **Information vs Narrative:** Are you drawn to charismatic founders and slick presentations? Do you check underlying data with rigorous scepticism?

5. **Recovering from Losses:** How do you analyse setbacks? Are you able to avoid blame shifting and extract valuable lessons for the future?

XI. CONFIRMATION BIAS

The Case of the Missing Counter-Arguments

Mark, a seasoned investigative journalist known for his impartiality, faced a dilemma in his latest project. He'd spent months delving into allegations of unethical practices within a powerful local corporation. The initial tip had triggered his instinctive desire to hold the powerful accountable.

As Mark burrowed deeper, he meticulously compiled evidence. Interviews with disgruntled former employees painted a damning picture of illegal waste disposal and financial cover-ups. A trove of leaked internal documents hinted at systemic disregard for safety regulations in pursuit of maximum profit. It felt like a textbook case of corporate criminality, begging for his scrutiny and eventual public exposure.

He'd even cultivated a tentative relationship with a current employee, Lily, who was willing to anonymously reveal further details. Each conversation brought new revelations, seemingly confirming Mark's initial suspicions.

Yet, in the spirit of fairness, Mark forced himself to seek the opposition's side. The official response from the corporation's management offered a vastly different narrative: disgruntled former employees with an axe to grind, misinterpreted communications blown out of proportion and a genuine commitment to abiding by industry standards. He noted several prominent local figures publicly vouching for the company's ethics and contribution to the community.

As the publication deadline loomed, Mark struggled to reconcile these competing versions of the truth. It wasn't about lack of evidence – with so much supporting his initial premise, he could comfortably publish a scathing exposé. However, an underlying unease lingered. Could he really ignore the company's rebuttals? Had he, despite his best intentions, focused solely on information that bolstered his existing storyline? The corporation had undeniably made generous charitable contributions to his city.

Ultimately, Mark chose a less inflammatory path. While not downplaying his findings, he included rebuttals, even though they felt flimsy next to the mountain of evidence against the corporation. He hoped readers would see through the corporate spin. However, initial responses proved disheartening. Some praised his tenacity, while others accused him of 'going soft' or being bought off. Mark began to second-guess himself. Had he really lost his edge or was the backlash just driven by local residents who were overly loyal to the corporation?

Confirmation Bias

Mark's struggle embodies the insidious power of confirmation bias: the tendency to seek out, favour and recall information that reinforces our preexisting beliefs, while downplaying or disregarding any contradictory evidence.

This bias operates subtly in various ways:

- **Selective Attention:** We pay more attention to details that fit our narrative. Even in a complex landscape of evidence, we can easily cherry-pick facts to create a sense of certainty.

- **Warped Interpretation:** Ambiguous statements or facts morph to justify our preconceptions. The same piece of evidence can often be framed to cast either guilt or innocence.

- **The Weight of 'First':** Our initial belief or hypothesis acts as an anchor, making it harder to give equal merit to information that arises afterwards.

- **Emotional Investment:** When a topic becomes deeply tied to our values, or a project consumes significant time, our need to be proven 'right' intensifies, distorting our judgement.

Confirmation bias has far-reaching consequences:

- **Missed Truths:** Tunnel vision blinds us to the bigger picture. Focusing on the corporation's flaws meant Mark may have neglected positive aspects that set them apart from industry rivals.

- **Perpetuating Divides:** Only seeking perspectives that support 'our side' fuels polarization, hinders genuine dialogue and makes finding solutions increasingly difficult.

- **Damage to Reputation:** A public accusation without adequately accounting for alternative views leaves you exposed to accusations of bias.

Questions for Self-Reflection

1. **Hidden Assumptions:** When starting a project, research or debate, identify your initial suspicions. How can you actively check those throughout the process?

2. **Devil's Advocate:** Can you create systems for deliberately exposing yourself to different viewpoints and seeking feedback from those likely to disagree with your conclusions?

3. **Alternative Interpretations:** Can you play a thought experiment to convincingly argue 'the other side'? Does that reveal weaknesses in your original stance?

4. **Nuance vs Polarization:** How can you foster the ability to acknowledge both the negative and positive traits of an individual, system or topic without feeling an emotional need to rigidly categorize it?

5. **Updating Beliefs:** When confronted with compelling counter-evidence, what are your internal strategies for gracefully shifting your position and not perceiving it as weakness but a strength?

XII. REPRESENTATIVE BIAS

The Illusion of the Ideal Salesperson

From his earliest days as a sales associate, Andrew harboured a vision of the ideal salesperson: extroverted, confident and armed with an effortless knack for building rapport. This archetype, constantly reinforced by pop culture and self-help gurus, occupied a firm spot in his mind. Consequently, even as he climbed the ranks to a managerial position, these preconceived notions continued to subtly shape his perceptions.

Then came the task of expanding his team. Two internal candidates stood out from the rest. Lisa, whose introspective manner belied her deep well of industry knowledge, meticulously researched client needs and tailored her approach accordingly. David, in contrast, exuded boisterous energy, possessed natural charisma and spoke eloquently about the power of forging client relationships.

A dissonance simmered within Andrew. Lisa's understanding of the product's technical details was impressive, a skill set he personally had always struggled to master. Yet, her reserved presentation style couldn't compete with the force of David's personality. David mirrored Andrew's idealized image of a salesperson so well that a connection was formed within moments of their first conversation. Despite her impressive resume, Lisa seemed to fade into the background.

Ultimately, David joined the team. Initially, his natural flair was a boon. Clients responded well to his enthusiasm, and the atmosphere within the team itself seemed to lighten. Watching David build immediate rapport fuelled Andrew's conviction that he'd made the right choice. The importance of this 'intangible' quality was something Andrew himself had championed within the company and now, here it was, embodied in this charismatic new hire.

As the months passed, however, cracks began to appear. While David's energy remained infectious, his sales numbers weren't consistently translating into closed deals. A nuanced understanding of the product was required to make strategic recommendations, but David struggled to retain technical details and became easily flustered when asked specific questions.

The deeper issue lay hidden beneath the surface. Whenever concerns were raised, whether with David directly or among the senior sales team, Andrew found himself subtly diverting the focus. He highlighted David's potential, emphasizing the power of relationships to secure future deals. His internal image of a 'successful salesperson' overrode a clear assessment of current results.

The situation reached breaking point after a significant deal with a key client fell through. On deeper investigation, it emerged that David's pitch had oversimplified the solution's limitations and capabilities. In his eagerness to please the client, he'd inadvertently set unrealistic expectations. Andrew found himself frustrated, questioning how he'd missed the warning signs – David's difficulty with product specifications and his aversion to detailed reports in favour of big-picture pronouncements.

The episode forced a shift in perspective. Andrew confronted a hidden truth: his own representative bias had subtly undermined his decision-making. The salesperson archetype he clung to placed outsized importance on charisma and undervalued the quiet technical mastery that Lisa so clearly possessed. He sought her input, finally valuing her perspective. Together, they crafted a multifaceted training plan for David, focused on balancing the 'art' of relationships with a rigorous foundation of knowledge.

Representative Bias

Andrew's experience offers a prime example of representative bias. This widespread cognitive trap is particularly insidious in investment settings. While relying on mental shortcuts and past patterns is often effective in navigating a fast-paced environment, representative bias causes us to overweight subjective pattern recognition while undervaluing nuanced context and quantifiable evidence that contradicts our expectations. Here's how it operates:

- **The Power of Prototypes:** Our brains favour easily recognized categories. Investors form prototypes (mental models) of 'winning' companies, 'innovative' CEOs and 'disruptive' industries. We seek familiar patterns as it's faster, easier and reassuring. While prototypes are useful starting points, over-reliance on them leads to missing signals that lie outside the pattern.

- **Stereotypes vs Substance:** Initial impressions can be misleading. Extroverted entrepreneurs might evoke the image of a visionary leader, but this can distract from their weaknesses. Conversely, unassuming personalities might mask deep analytical skills and a grasp of crucial market forces. Stereotypes cloud our evaluations.

- **The Narratives We Tell Ourselves:** Humans are susceptible to well-constructed narratives, particularly from charismatic communicators. A compelling story around a product or CEO might eclipse rigorous due diligence, creating unwarranted optimism. A focus on style over substance is exacerbated by representative bias: if the pitch 'feels' like success, we assume it *is* success.

There are some specific consequences of this bias for investors:

- **Lost Opportunities:** Bias towards a certain investor 'type' might cause us to overlook unconventional yet highly effective founders. Similarly, startups in unglamorous sectors with deep, long-term potential might be dismissed if they don't match our expectations of success being driven by 'hot' new concepts.

- **FOMO-Driven Errors:** When an asset or opportunity aligns neatly with our preconceptions of what 'success' looks like, a misplaced fear of missing out (FOMO) can rush investors into decisions without deep analysis. This often fuels speculative bubbles driven as much by perception as fundamentals.

- **Ignoring Warning Signs:** Representative bias can blind investors to subtle but crucial indicators of trouble. A CEO's bold announcements could overshadow concerns raised by the

CTO, or a startup's social media buzz might drown out questions about their scalability and business model.

Recognizing representative bias is only the first step. Here are some active countermeasures you can take:

- **Diverse Teams:** A range of educational backgrounds, investing styles and personality types helps to counter groupthink. Dissenting voices are less likely to be dismissed when diversity is built into the investment team itself.

- **Contrarian Indicators:** Actively seek out data points and perspectives that challenge your initial assessment or go against market hype. Assign a 'devil's advocate' role within the team to focus specifically on contrarian evidence.

- **Beware of the Sunk Cost Fallacy:** If an investment shows signs of failing to live up to initial expectations, the amount you've already put into the trade can make letting go of it psychologically difficult. The sunk cost fallacy compounds representative bias.

- **Emphasize Data Over Impressions:** Develop processes favouring measurable outcomes over initial 'fit'. Implement anonymous reviews for pitches to combat personal biases.

Questions for Self-Reflection

1. **Stereotypes and First Impressions:** Have you formed stereotypical impressions of people based on their appearance,

mannerisms or background? How has that influenced your judgments?

2. **Style Over Substance:** Are there situations where you often place greater value on confidence and charisma over demonstrable results or expertise?

3. **Qualifications vs Potential:** When selecting between a 'safe' choice based on qualifications vs a riskier yet promising choice based on their fit with an idealized type, how do you proceed?

4. **Evidence-Based Assessments:** What safeguards can you put in place to ensure your assessments remain rooted in concrete evidence and skills rather than stereotypes?

XIII. THE CLUSTERING ILLUSION

The Mirage of Hidden Insights

Sarah, a seasoned market analyst, was poring over sales data for a retail chain's stores across the country. On the surface, performance seemed largely even, with sales varying within predictable ranges. But Sarah was relentless in searching for underlying patterns that might signal opportunities for targeted marketing or inventory adjustments. She layered on additional data – demographics, weather patterns, local economic indexes – hunting for clues within the vast dataset.

One afternoon, there was a glimmer of a potential breakthrough. Clustering emerged in specific geographic regions: seemingly random bursts of significantly higher-than-average sales alongside dips in nearby stores. Was this evidence of untapped consumer trends? Could her insight unlock increased efficiency or identify underserved markets? Excitement swelled in Sarah as she envisioned presenting her findings to the company's executives, her analysis propelling her career forward.

Driven by this promising lead, Sarah began digging deeper. She focused on stores within 'outperforming' clusters, seeking commonalities. Product mix, local competitor activity, even seemingly trivial variables like parking and store layout were meticulously investigated. Her initial burst of confidence faded slowly, replaced by a creeping sense of uncertainty. No discernible pattern emerged to connect the high-performing stores; there was no hidden thread to justify the clusters.

Could her data be wrong? Could her meticulous analysis somehow be flawed?

Seeking an outside perspective, Sarah enlisted the help of a statistician colleague. With fresh eyes, they scrutinized the dataset and Sarah's methodology. After several checks, the conclusion became clear: the clusters were just that, groups born of pure chance. While patterns often exist, especially in large datasets, it's vital to differentiate true correlation from inevitable random anomalies. The human need to seek order in chaos had tripped Sarah up.

From that moment on, Sarah's perspective changed. She didn't abandon her keen eye for anomalies; instead, she now armed it with a deeper statistical understanding. The quest for patterns remained, but it no longer dominated. Rather, it became a starting point for verifying correlations against probabilities. Data and intuition could now work in concert, helping her see past the deceptive simplicity of a cluster to its true meaning.

The Clustering Illusion

Sarah's experience is a prime example of the clustering illusion. This cognitive bias makes us perceive patterns within random distributions of data, events or phenomena. This desire to find meaning in randomness arises from several factors:

- **Apophenia - The Need for Order:** Our brains are wired to find patterns, a skill vital for learning and understanding complex processes. However, this same pattern-seeking tendency can lead us to perceive correlations and cause-effect relationships where none exist.

- **Focus on Confirmation and Blindness to the 'Ordinary':** When focused on finding something exceptional, it's easy to magnify the importance of unusual clusters while overlooking the ordinary, less noticeable 'background noise' within the data. This focus heightens our chance of mistaking anomalies for insights.

- **Small Sample Sizes:** Especially when starting with small datasets, a few clustered deviations can appear significant, leading decision-makers away from more rigorous statistical analysis. Larger sets often reveal that these are within an expected range of variation.

The clustering illusion can have a negative impact on your investment decision-making process.

- **Wasted Resources:** Acting on misidentified patterns can lead to misallocated funds, misplaced focus and ineffective campaigns. In Sarah's case, this almost led to hyper-analysis of random clusters, a significant expenditure of time and resources.

- **Ignoring True Causal Factors:** Obsessing over the wrong patterns can divert attention from what is genuinely driving a situation. Identifying the real trends relies on filtering out random 'noise'.

- **Overconfidence in Intuition:** Intuiting patterns without a foundation of rigorous analysis can create a false sense of certainty. We must balance intuition with objective assessment methods.

Awareness of the clustering illusion isn't about becoming cynical. Here's how to harness this knowledge:

- **Seek Statistical Expertise:** Consultation with statistical experts early on can help you to identify true patterns or validate suspected trends, guiding resource allocation effectively.

- **Widen the Context:** When faced with apparent clusters, expand your data collection. Do these patterns remain when including more items, a longer time frame or unrelated factors? Are they still significant in terms of the broader trends?

- **Beware the Seduction of Simplicity:** The clustering illusion thrives on seemingly clear patterns. If your conclusion relies heavily on 'aha!' moments rather than careful calculation, reexamine for random variance.

Questions for Self-Reflection

1. **Misinterpreting Data Patterns:** Can you recall a time when you identified a pattern or trend in data, only to find out, later, that it was based on too limited a sample or random variations?

2. **Pattern Seeking vs Statistical Rigour:** Do you lean more towards seeking patterns (and possible meaning) within data

or thorough statistical analysis that eliminates random correlations?

3. **Navigating Data Uncertainty:** When facing uncertainty or a potentially chaotic set of data points, what steps do you take to prevent yourself from being misled by the patterns you perceive?

4. **Insight vs Evidence in Team Decisions:** In team decision-making, how do you balance valuing insights gained from pattern recognition with the demand for a statistically verifiable explanation?

XIV. HINDSIGHT BIAS

I Knew It

Julia, a veteran market analyst, built her reputation on a seemingly keen ability to see around corners. Years of poring over economic indicators, unravelling industry trends and meticulously weighing historical data had honed her razor-sharp analytical skills. Clients valued her ability to not only interpret the present but to envision likely market directions. During strategy sessions, the room crackled with anticipation when Julia outlined potential scenarios, her confidence as compelling as the charts and statistics she wielded.

These moments were undeniably thrilling. More than simply being right, Julia enjoyed the intellectual satisfaction of her predictions playing out with sometimes startling accuracy. It felt like proof of her exceptional abilities, cementing her status within a firm whose competitive culture rewarded boldness and prized predictive success. Yet, the seeds of a nagging unease began to take root. Was this uncanny foresight genuinely the product of superior skill, or were unseen forces colouring her perceptions?

Then came a particularly volatile period. Julia invested weeks tracking a commodity market whose inherent fluctuations would test even the most seasoned analyst. Every price shift, news item and policy statement fuelled a swirling mass of conflicting indicators. Yet, even in this chaotic environment, she felt a strong undercurrent pulling her towards a specific prediction. Complex trade tensions, coupled with geopolitical posturing, seemed to converge in a way that screamed 'imminent spike!' Initially, Julia wavered, plagued by her own mental counter-arguments. However, with every meeting in which she voiced this increasingly strong conviction, the resistance faded. Soon, Julia felt almost giddy with excitement. This was what separated her from the cautious bunch of mere 'data crunchers'.

When the predicted spike did happen, with almost breathtaking abruptness, elation soared through her. Yet, the sense of triumph had an uncomfortable edge that Julia couldn't quite define. This high-wire prediction had made her the talk of the firm, and she'd secured a potential high-value deal based on the assumption this uptrend would hold. Then, as is often the case with any volatile market, the inevitable reversal kicked in. An unforeseen disaster hit supply chains, causing prices to plunge beyond anyone's projections. That seemingly brilliant win transformed into an ugly red stain on her carefully cultivated record.

This reversal shook Julia deeply. Had she arrogantly ignored signs that didn't align with the narrative she was selling herself and others? In reviewing her meticulous notes, she discovered a worrying pattern: while documenting potential variables, her predictions focused almost obsessively on a single outcome, as if willing it into existence. The discomfort morphed into a deeper crisis when she realized she genuinely couldn't remember the simmering doubts she'd had at the start, recorded in black and white.

With humility replacing hubris, Julia sought fresh insight. Consulting a former professor specializing in behavioural economics, she uncovered the culprit: hindsight bias. While in its insidious grip, she'd unknowingly rewritten the script. She'd celebrated her moments of foresight that had proven partially accurate, but she'd also unconsciously downplayed the doubts and alternative scenarios that had populated her original thinking. It was a harsh dose of reality - humbling yet empowering. For true knowledge to triumph over delusion, she realized she must dissect not just her victories but her thought processes themselves.

Hindsight Bias

Julia's struggle illustrates the potent ways hindsight bias – the 'knew-it-all-along' effect – warps our understanding of past events. This phenomenon isn't about lying to ourselves. Rather, our natural tendency to find logical patterns causes us to subtly and subconsciously reshape our memory of a prediction when an outcome later becomes obvious. Several specific mechanisms fuel this distortion:

- **Craving Coherence:** Our brains struggle with randomness. Even complex or chaotic situations feel more controllable if they align with a simple narrative arc. When we look back after we know the outcome, we prune away details that don't fit neatly, exaggerating the elements that seem to have predicted what happened.

- **Overemphasizing Success, Filtering Out 'Misses':** When an expected outcome materializes (even partially), we're flooded with the validation of 'being right'. Our focus narrows intensely on confirming evidence, overshadowing any original uncertainties or less obvious potential paths. Meanwhile, we conveniently lose track of predictions that ultimately proved inaccurate.

- **The Seductive Narrative:** With every retelling of our 'prescient' analysis, the 'knew it' story strengthens. The original thought process gets streamlined in hindsight, edited into a more impressive version than the messy, sometimes contradictory reality.

Hindsight bias doesn't simply hurt analysts' reputations. Its deceptive tendrils infiltrate everyday life from boardrooms to historical narratives:

- **Medical Misdiagnosis:** A doctor focused on an initial hypothesis may, upon later finding they were wrong, unconsciously rewrite their memory of early patient interactions. They may create the illusion they considered a broader range of potential diagnoses or noticed crucial red flags at the start that now seem obvious (but weren't at the time).

- **The Justice System:** Jurors hearing evidence after a verdict is reached can fall prey to distorting their recollection of specific testimony in a similar way. Hindsight clouds their true memory of how certain they were of a decision before the trial concluded. This can impact not only verdicts but perceptions of due process fairness.

- **Historical Narratives:** The 'winners write history' adage rings true in part due to this bias. Leaders, reflecting on successful campaigns, victories or societal shifts, often overstate their certainty of those outcomes, diminishing the impact of luck, timing and other variables that were genuinely unpredictable at the time.

While recognizing the bias is crucial, truly combating its effects requires more than just awareness:

- **Documentation as a Safeguard:** Before a prediction becomes 'set', capture it alongside known ambiguities and alternative scenarios. Avoid vague statements, forcing specificity upon both what you see as likely *and* acknowledging its limits. This provides us with a tool to later challenge our memory's slippery nature.

- **Premortem Analysis:** Imagine your decision or assessment failed spectacularly. This uncomfortable mental exercise helps to counteract the focus on positive results that fuels hindsight bias. Conduct this before an outcome is known, and document those anticipated failure points.

- **Diverse and Contradictory Inputs:** Actively seek information that challenges your initial hypothesis. In teams, encourage a 'devil's advocate' approach rather than quick consensus that shuts down dissenting views before their true value is considered.

Questions for Self-Reflection

1. **Memory Distortion and Certainty:** Describe an incident where your memory of a decision was that you were sure of the outcome but, upon talking to friends or colleagues, you realize

that there was actually some nuance and uncertainty at the time. Now, think of a case where the opposite applies – you had much clearer convictions about a decision than you later recall.

2. **Judging Others:** Are there situations where hindsight bias leads to unfairly harsh judgements of others, looking at their past choices through the lens of knowledge you only possess in the present?

3. **Mitigating Hindsight Bias:** What specific measures have you found most effective in combating hindsight bias, both in yourself and in the decision-making of those around you?

XV. RECENCY BIAS

A Change of Pace

Alex wasn't one to get rattled. A decade of high-stakes analysis had forged an analytical mind immune to market jitters or the overenthusiasm of rookie investors. His niche focus? Unlocking the potential within 'value stocks' – fundamentally sound companies trading below their true worth because they were being overshadowed by the latest market darlings. This approach had earned him both a strong reputation and more than a few satisfied clients.

Alex was spotting patterns of innovation in seemingly stagnant industries. Old-line manufacturers had revamped R&D divisions and shipping behemoths were quietly investing in data analytics to streamline logistics. These were signals the market was missing. And nowhere was this trend more pronounced than in his latest target: GlobalCom.

The telecom giant was a byword for stability, not sizzle. But Alex saw something else. Buried beneath the predictable quarterly reports were signs of a long-term investment cycle. GlobalCom was buying up smaller fibre-optic networks in emerging markets and partnering with satellite internet providers – moves towards expanding infrastructure that hinted at a strategic pivot. This could be the catalyst for major growth in the coming years... if his thesis was right.

Initially, the pitch to his senior team had been met with polite indifference. 'GlobalCom? Safe dividend stock for retirees, not exactly high potential' one portfolio manager countered. Yet, after weeks of persistent nudging from Alex and a begrudging acceptance that his data couldn't be ignored, a tentative decision was made for a small strategic buy. It wasn't the full-throated endorsement Alex had hoped for, but it was a start.

Then, it happened. Front-page news: 'GlobalCom announces a mega-merger with a leading AI software firm'. Suddenly, industry analysts were singing GlobalCom's praises, using phrases like, 'a visionary move,' and, 'poised for dominance in the 5G revolution'. Almost overnight, his stodgy stock pick became a target for every portfolio manager trying to claim they'd seen it coming all along.

It should have been a moment of triumph for Alex. Instead, a sense of unease ate away at him. Was the initial scepticism his idea met with correct – had he simply gotten lucky? His model still pointed to the long play, suggesting that GlobalCom's true value lay in its underlying groundwork – this merger was flashy, but would it expedite or hinder the strategy Alex envisioned?

Then came the client calls. They wanted more GlobalCom, and they wanted it now. Some demanded they pivot further from a value-focus to ride the momentum. Alex's warnings about the dangers of herd mentality and the need for a balanced approach were drowned out in the clamour for the next big thing.

Recency Bias

Recency bias is the insidious belief that what happens most recently matters more than a broader historical view or a well-considered long-term strategy. Its impact on investors is significant:

- **The Science:** Psychological studies reveal our tendency to update our mental models based on the latest happenings rather than integrating new information carefully. News is particularly powerful – its immediacy and accompanying visuals create a vividness that anchors itself in our minds more strongly than, say, a spreadsheet filed away months before. Importantly, the emotions elicited by news – be it excitement or fear – further distort our thinking, making us prone to impulsive investment choices.

- **Examples:** Beyond the obvious examples of the rush to chase recent winners or panic selling in a downturn, recency bias has a subtler side:

    o   Overestimating a company's ability to consistently innovate based on its one recent hot product launch.

    o   Giving too much weight to a political leader's latest pronouncements on trade or taxation without considering a country's broader economic picture.

    o   Bailing out of an industry due to recent negative press cycles while ignoring the potential for long-term recovery and undervalued opportunities.

- **Effects:** Recency bias leads to a reactive investor mindset, where emotions dictate the strategy rather than the other way around. It erodes discipline, encouraging decisions based on what's hot now rather than what makes fundamental sense. Long-term investments get jettisoned in the face of short-term shocks, while investors may chase fads instead of sticking to time-tested principles of diversification and sound valuation.

Questions for Self-Reflection

1. **Emotional Bias:** Could the excitement or worry generated by a recent event be distorting your perception of the overall investment opportunity?

2. **Misinterpreting Price Fluctuations:** Are you in danger of confusing a short-term price bump with a fundamental shift in a company's value proposition?

3. **The Influence of FOMO:** Is fear of missing out (or fear of losses) causing you to rush into a decision before fully examining all the evidence?

4. **Aligning Decisions with Data, Not Headlines:** Have you ever neglected historical data or your own initial judgment calls because they don't align with the headlines of the moment?

5. **The Value of External Perspectives:** Have you considered a 'sanity check' with a trusted colleague when you're looking to act quickly on new information? This may provide a different perspective and counterbalance your emotional state.

XVI. SELF-SERVING BIAS

The Star Analyst

Marcus leaned back in his chair, feeling a rush of triumph. His presentation was a hit. Charts lit up the big screen, showcasing the bold investments he'd spearheaded. Graphs told an enticing story – a spike in returns, outperforming the benchmark and justifying his 'go big or go home' approach. Clients were practically eating out of his hand; it didn't even matter that one portfolio in his pitch held a somewhat riskier than usual stake in a promising new tech startup.

As the Q&A began, a seasoned investor raised a concern. 'Marcus, interesting choice there with Evermore Systems. Seems a bit volatile for this client profile.'

Marcus bristled inwardly but flashed his most dazzling smile. 'Volatility can be a sign of untapped opportunity', he argued, launching into a carefully rehearsed spiel about Evermore's disruptive potential. Besides, with those projected numbers from his sector analysis, surely a little gamble would pay off for his client and boost his own reputation in the long run.

Later, sipping celebratory drinks with a few junior analysts, Marcus basked in their admiration. 'That old-timer wouldn't know real potential if it hit him in the face', he scoffed, relishing his successful deflection of criticism. In those heady moments, there was no shadow of doubt in his mind. He was talented. He'd earned this success.

Over the following weeks, unease began to gnaw at him. But this was easily attributed to the market's general turbulence. Sure, Evermore was experiencing the odd drop, but Marcus refused to budge from his thesis. In fact, he'd doubled down, even slightly increasing his client's holding on a promising hunch. This was how fortunes were made – holding firm in the face of temporary setbacks. Yet, when the news broke about Evermore's key patent dispute, his confidence faltered.

Weeks turned into months and Evermore's stock didn't bounce back – quite the opposite. Client complaints, once muted worries via email, escalated into angry calls. While Marcus scrambled to manage the fallout, a bitter thought began to snake through his mind – perhaps he had been overconfident, misjudging his own 'genius', or rather, mistaking luck for brilliance.

Self-Serving Bias

Self-serving bias is a cognitive distortion that plays a critical role in how individuals interpret their successes and failures, shaping their sense of self and their interactions with the world. This bias is deeply embedded in the human psyche, serving both to protect self-esteem and to maintain a coherent self-narrative. Its manifestations are widespread, influencing behaviour in personal, professional and social contexts.

At the heart of self-serving bias are two primary psychological drives:

- **Self-Esteem Protection:** Humans have an innate desire to see themselves positively and maintain high self-esteem. Acknowledging personal flaws or admitting to failures can be psychologically damaging, so individuals often attribute negative outcomes to external factors to preserve their self-image.

- **Cognitive Consistency:** People strive for consistency in their beliefs and perceptions, including their self-perception. Admitting to shortcomings or failures introduces cognitive dissonance, a state of mental discomfort when one holds contradictory beliefs. Self-serving bias helps to resolve this dissonance by reconciling failures with a positive self-view.

Self-serving bias manifests in various aspects of life, illustrating its pervasive influence:

- **Academic Performance:** Students attribute good grades to their intelligence and hard work but blame poor grades on external factors, such as the difficulty of the exam or inadequate instruction.

- **Professional Settings:** Employees view promotions or successes as the result of their competencies, while attributing setbacks or criticisms to external factors, such as office politics or market conditions.

- **Interpersonal Relationships:** In conflicts or relationship issues, individuals often see their actions as justified or driven by circumstances, while attributing negative outcomes to the other person's character flaws or intentions.

While self-serving bias serves protective functions, its implications can be far-reaching and not always positive:

- **Impaired Learning and Growth:** By externalizing blame and internalizing success, individuals may fail to learn from their mistakes, hindering personal and professional growth.

- **Interpersonal Conflict:** This bias can lead to misunderstandings and conflicts, as individuals fail to acknowledge their role in negative outcomes, potentially damaging relationships.

- **Organizational Dynamics:** In a workplace, self-serving bias can contribute to a culture of blame, reducing accountability and undermining teamwork and collaboration.

Addressing self-serving bias involves fostering greater self-awareness and promoting a culture of openness and accountability:

- **Reflective Practices:** Engaging in regular self-reflection and seeking feedback can help individuals recognize and adjust for their biases.

- **Cultivating a Growth Mindset:** Embracing challenges and failures as opportunities for learning can shift the perspective from protecting self-esteem to valuing personal development.

- **Encouraging Accountability:** In organizational settings, creating environments where mistakes are viewed as learning opportunities can reduce the need to externalize blame.

Self-serving bias underscores the complexity of human cognition and the lengths to which individuals will go to maintain a positive self-image. Recognizing and mitigating this bias can lead to more honest self-assessment, improved personal growth and healthier interpersonal and professional relationships. By confronting the self-serving bias, individuals and organizations can foster a culture of accountability, resilience and continuous improvement.

Questions for Self-Reflection

1. **Objective Self-Reflection:** After a win, are you prone to exaggerating your own role, minimizing others' contributions or ignoring a bit of fortuitous timing?

2. **Response to Failure:** Does a failure trigger anger towards colleagues or external circumstances rather than honest reflection on your own contribution to the problem?

3. **Reception to Constructive Criticism:** Are you reluctant to embrace constructive criticism, seeing it as a personal attack rather than an opportunity to grow?

4. **Leadership in Addressing Setbacks:** When discussing setbacks with your team, do you model personal accountability or default to scapegoating and finding culprits?

5. **Evaluating Team Members' Abilities:** Does your assessment of others' abilities shift depending on the success or failure of a task? Do you consider someone incompetent if things go wrong but laud them as a genius when things go right?

XVII. THE SUNK COST FALLACY

The Legacy Project

Sarah couldn't mask her apprehension as she approached the conference room. It had been five years – five long years – since she'd been handed the 'Prestige' project. Back then, as a rising star in project management, it had felt like a breakthrough opportunity. Prestige was meant to be her masterpiece: a complete revamp of the company's aging supply chain software. Its success would not just mean smoother operations; it would vault Sarah into the upper echelons of leadership within the logistics giant.

Of course, things hadn't unfolded quite as the initial brochures promised. The 'simple' integration with existing systems turned into a nightmare of unpicking outdated architecture and endless compatibility conflicts. Key vendors pulled out at the last minute, forcing frantic scrambles for replacements. What was budgeted as a two-year initiative was still dragging on, each quarter bringing fresh delays and revised budget numbers that far exceeded anything Sarah had ever been responsible for.

As she entered the room filled with weary board members and tight-lipped senior executives, a wave of exhaustion threatened to overpower her usual practiced composure. Her meticulous and polished slides, outlining a new phase of custom development to salvage the project, felt oddly disconnected from how she felt inside. Out of the corner of her eye, she caught her worried frown lines reflected in the window. This wasn't just a presentation anymore; this was a reckoning.

'Sarah', the CEO began, his tone flat and a little cool, 'I think we all agree that Prestige hasn't lived up to its name. Let's cut to the chase. Your new proposal asks for another hefty resource injection, with only vague estimates of when, or if, we'll see a usable product.'

That familiar tightness settled in her chest. Each objection was justified, yet to accept them, to walk away now, would be to admit something Sarah struggled to put into words, even within the privacy of her own mind: failure. Five years of her career, countless sleepless nights and frayed relationships, all for this?

A younger Sarah might have been swayed by the clarity of this stark truth. This Sarah, however, the one weathered by countless firefighting missions to rescue Prestige, instead clung to what she perceived as battle-hardened logic.

'I wouldn't be here if this were unsalvageable', she countered, her voice strong even as that internal doubt lingered. 'We've invested too much to stop now. This custom solution addresses issues none of the off-the-shelf options could. It's…it's the only way to protect our existing operations.'

And there it was – the phrase she'd unknowingly relied on far too many times in recent years.

The Sunk Cost Fallacy

The sunk cost fallacy embodies one of the most pervasive and counterproductive cognitive biases in decision-making, affecting individuals, businesses and governments alike. It illustrates how our past investment in something can make it difficult to accept the idea of cutting our losses, unduly influencing current and future decisions and leading to a continuation of unprofitable actions or projects.

The sunk cost fallacy arises from several psychological phenomena:

- **Loss Aversion:** This is a principle of behavioural economics that suggests losses are perceived as significantly more painful than gains are pleasurable. This aversion to realizing losses can compel individuals to continue investing in a losing proposition in the hope of turning it around.

- **Cognitive Dissonance:** This psychological discomfort arises from holding two conflicting beliefs simultaneously, such as believing oneself to be a good decision-maker while facing evidence of a poor decision. To reduce dissonance, individuals may irrationally continue investing in a losing project rather than acknowledging their mistake.

- **Completion Bias:** This is the human desire to see tasks or projects to completion, regardless of their current utility or success. This bias can make it psychologically challenging to abandon projects that are near completion, even when it's logical to do so.

- **Confirmation Bias:** This is the tendency to search for, interpret, favour and recall information in a way that confirms one's preexisting beliefs or hypotheses. This can lead to overvaluing evidence that supports continuing with the investment and undervaluing evidence that suggests selling it.

The sunk cost fallacy has broad implications across various domains:

- **Personal Finance:** Individuals may continue investing in declining stocks or persist with expensive hobbies that no longer provide satisfaction simply because of the amount they've already spent.

- **Business Strategy:** Companies may continue to fund failing projects or products due to significant prior investment, leading to further losses and misallocation of resources.

- **Public Policy:** Governments might persist with costly infrastructure or military projects well beyond the point of viability, motivated by the desire to justify their initial expenditure.

Addressing the sunk cost fallacy requires both awareness of its influence and active strategies to counteract its effects:

- **Pre-Decisional Accountability:** Establishing mechanisms for accountability before making investment decisions can help ensure that decisions are revisited and evaluated objectively.

- **Separation of Decision Makers:** Rotating project leaders or involving third parties in review processes can help provide a fresh perspective unburdened by knowledge of past investment.

- **Emphasis on Data-Driven Decisions:** Cultivating a culture that values decisions based on current data and future prospects rather than past expenditures can help mitigate the fallacy.

- **Fostering a Learning Culture:** Encouraging an environment where mistakes are viewed as learning opportunities can reduce the psychological barriers to acknowledging and rectifying poor past decisions.

The sunk cost fallacy represents a significant challenge to rational decision-making, driven by deep-seated psychological tendencies and cognitive biases. By recognizing and actively addressing these biases, individuals and organizations can make more objective decisions, optimize resource allocation and minimize unnecessary losses. Understanding and overcoming the sunk cost fallacy is crucial for fostering resilience, innovation and long-term success in an ever-changing environment.

Questions for Self-Reflection

1. **Prioritizing Quality over Completion:** Do you place more value on 'finishing' a project, even if you anticipate subpar results, than pivoting to an entirely new and more promising strategy?

2. **Beyond Binary Decisions:** Have you ever framed decisions too narrowly (continue or kill), ignoring more nuanced options that don't conform to the initial vision i.e., to scale back or dramatically change a project's scope?

3. **Objective Analysis of Options:** When evaluating options, do you create detailed projections considering past costs *and* future resource needs for each pathway, or does sentiment about past efforts taint your judgement?

4. **The Fear of Being Wrong:** Is the fear of appearing wrong (in past judgment calls) influencing your current stance more than what genuinely serves the best interests of the company?

5. **Encouraging Constructive Feedback:** When seeking team input, do you foster a culture where raising issues with an ongoing project is lauded (proactive problem-solving), or is dissent subtly punished (perceived as lack of dedication)?

XVIII. THE AVAILABILITY HEURISTIC

Eye on the Newsfeed

Liam's finger hovered over the 'post' button, but something held him back. As the founder of a social media analytics company, he knew better than most how fast an idea could gain traction – or get consumed by an online firestorm. Yet, that usually applied to his clients' content, not his own controversial take on the current state of the market.

For weeks, he'd wrestled with the growing certainty that investors and entrepreneurs alike were blinded by a dangerous mix of recession panic and tech bubble delusion. On the one hand, the numbers told a worrying story. Venture capital funding was indeed drying up and hyped-up startups were making messy layoffs. Every new article and doom-laden prediction by a finance influencer chipped away at the 'anything is fundable if you pitch it right' optimism that defined the recent boom. To Liam, posting his contrarian 'back to fundamentals' thesis could be a much-needed reality check...or professional suicide. His personal brand was built on positivity; he was the eternal tech enthusiast cheering on the next big thing.

'You need to say something', his wife, Maria, had argued a few nights ago over a tense dinner. Her usual unwavering support now carried an undeniable edge of concern. With her job in finance suddenly shaky, and with both their savings sunk into his company, she wasn't just his emotional sounding board anymore. His next steps could entail very real risk for both of them. Yet, even under these pressures, Liam's core belief was unshakeable – the current wave of market negativity was disproportionate to the reality. There was a huge opportunity waiting for those who were willing to invest in the long game.

Then, after yet another barrage of headlines about tech giants shedding jobs, something in him snapped. He took the leap and published a series of posts carefully balancing stark data with an equally forceful optimism. His argument? Yes, a correction was hitting hard, and those investments built on shaky foundations would indeed crumble. But it was also a moment of ruthless market efficiency that would clear the clutter and make room for fresh ideas solving real-world problems with sustainable business models. His call to action cut through the noise: 'Stop obsessing about the fear cycle and start building. Now is when true grit wins'. He closed his laptop and took a deep breath.

The Availability Heuristic

The availability heuristic is a cognitive shortcut that significantly shapes our perception of reality, our decision-making process and judgments about the world around us. This heuristic involves the tendency to base decisions on information that is more readily available to us rather than all possible information. This bias can dramatically influence personal behaviours, business strategies and even societal norms.

First defined by psychologists Amos Tversky and Daniel Kahneman, the availability heuristic is part of the duo's groundbreaking work in identifying the systematic errors in human thought processes. The heuristic operates on a simple principle: if something can be recalled easily, we feel it must be important or at least more common than alternatives that are not as readily recalled. This mental shortcut is influenced by several factors:

- **Recency and Frequency:** Recent events or frequently encountered information is easier to recall and, therefore, often seen as more significant or common.

- **Vividness and Emotion:** Events or information that is emotionally charged or particularly vivid are more easily remembered and can disproportionately influence our judgment.

- **Media and Social Amplification:** Media exposure shapes what information is accessible to us, with sensationalized or negative news often being more readily available and memorable.

The availability heuristic has wide-ranging implications across various aspects of life and society:

- **Risk Perception:** Individuals may overestimate the likelihood of dramatic but rare events (e.g., plane crashes) over more common but less sensational risks (e.g., car accidents), due to the former being more prominent in the media.

- **Investment Decisions:** Investors might judge the health of the stock market based on the most recent headlines or high-profile stories, leading to decisions that are not grounded in comprehensive market analysis.

- **Business Strategy:** Companies may prioritize strategic initiatives based on what competitors' activities have received the most attention, rather than on a balanced assessment of all competitive threats and opportunities.

To counteract the influence of the availability heuristic, several strategies can be employed:

- **Diverse Information Sources:** Actively seeking out information from a variety of sources can help ensure a more balanced view that is not overly influenced by the most recent or high-profile news.

- **Statistical Literacy:** Understanding and applying statistical principles can help individuals recognize when their judgments may be unduly influenced by easily recalled examples rather than by the actual data.

- **Critical Thinking and Scepticism:** Developing the habit of critically evaluating the source and relevance of information can mitigate the impact of compelling but potentially misleading information.

- **Awareness and Reflection:** Simply being aware of the availability heuristic and its effects can help individuals question their intuitive judgments and consider whether they are based on a comprehensive set of information.

The availability heuristic underscores the complex interplay between cognition, emotion and behaviour. By recognizing the ways in which easily recalled information can bias our perceptions and decisions, individuals and organizations can take steps to ensure that their actions are based on a more complete and accurate understanding of the world. Developing strategies to mitigate the influence of the availability heuristic is crucial for making more informed decisions, whether in our personal lives, in business strategy in or public policy.

Questions for Self-Reflection

1. **Counter-argument and Data Collection Strategies:** Before a major decision, do you actively solicit perspectives that counter what the majority seem fixated on? Do you have processes to ensure broad data gathering rather than just relying on what hits your inbox?

2. **Anecdotes vs Larger Context:** Are you easily swayed by recent anecdotes, forgetting the larger context (i.e., does your neighbour's terrible experience with a contractor stop you from using them when their broader track record is positive)?

3. **Balancing Perceptions with Success Stories:** When negativity looms, do you make an extra effort to seek 'success stories' relevant to the situation to ensure your perception is balanced?

4. **Objective Evaluation of New Policies:** After implementing a new policy or practice, do you include clear-eyed 'check-in' points where success metrics can be evaluated so you aren't swayed by more immediately noticeable failures? This minimizes a kneejerk reaction driven by the availability heuristic.

5. **Cultivating a Critical Work Culture:** Have you built a work culture where challenging doomsday thinking driven by the 'news of the day' is rewarded in team decision-making?

XIX. THE IKEA EFFECT

The Pride of Assembly

Sarah and Mark stood back, surveying their work with a mix of exhaustion and satisfaction. The once chaotic tangle of wooden panels, cryptic diagrams and alarmingly numerous tiny screws had somehow been transformed into a sturdy, if slightly misaligned, bookshelf. It wasn't the sleek piece they'd initially admired in a design magazine, but after hours of bickering over the instructions, followed by a frantic hunt for a mysteriously missing Allen wrench, it felt deeply theirs.

'Not bad, considering', Sarah declared, giving the bookshelf a tentative pat. Its imperfections – including the faint smudge where Mark had spilled coffee in a bout of diagram-induced frustration – seemed only to add to its character.

Mark grinned. 'Honestly, that was harder than it had any right to be. Think we deserve takeaway tonight as DIY superstars.' Later, amidst scattered tools and sawdust, they'd laugh about their ordeal, declaring the misshapen bookcase a symbol of their resilience.

This sense of disproportionate pride over a rather unremarkable piece of furniture wasn't entirely rational. But Sarah, a usually pragmatic marketing executive, knew this wasn't simply about saving money; they could have found something comparable that was pre-assembled. Nor was it just shared triumph in a battle against confusing diagrams. There was something else – a lingering warmth and attachment that wouldn't have existed had they simply clicked 'order' online.

The IKEA Effect

The IKEA effect is a fascinating cognitive bias where we place a disproportionately high value on products we've partially or fully created ourselves. The name stems from the iconic Swedish retailer, famous for its flat-pack furniture that necessitates assembly by the buyer, often with considerable effort. The experience of self-assembly becomes subtly woven into our perception of the final product, inflating its worth in our eyes.

But it's not just about furniture. While the name references a specific brand and type of labour, the IKEA effect manifests in all areas of life:

- o The pride a home chef feels dishing up a complex recipe, even when the results aren't objectively restaurant-quality.

- o The attachment someone feels to a simple website they built using a DIY template vs hiring a professional for a more polished outcome.

- o The exaggerated delight a child takes in painting a wobbly ceramic sculpture, likely far exceeding how they'd feel about a store-bought masterpiece.

The term 'the IKEA effect' was coined in a 2011 study by Michael I. Norton of Harvard Business School, along with Daniel Mochon and Dan Ariely. Their research demonstrated several points:

- Participants consistently overvalued their own amateurish origami creations compared to the work of experts, as well as pre-folded offerings.
- When asked how much others would value their work, this bias disappeared. Participants grasped their creations weren't as impressive as they felt.
- The longer and more arduous the assembly process, the stronger the inflation of perceived value, confirming the link between effort and bias intensity.

Psychologists link the IKEA effect to several interconnected factors:

- **Effort Justification:** Our brains have a built-in desire for consistency. After significant effort investment, we want to see something positive as an outcome to 'justify' that exertion. Thus, downplaying a self-assembled item's imperfections and inflating its value becomes necessary.
- **The Endowment Effect:** This well-studied bias shows that we overvalue things simply because we feel ownership, even without labour involved. This compounds the IKEA effect – once an item is 'ours', our labour further solidifies that biased valuation.
- **Competence Boost:** Whether actual mastery is the outcome of assembly or not, the mere act of completing a task fuels a sense of competence and mastery that increases feelings of attachment.
- **Emotional and Sensory Cues:** The physical act of creating engages touch, sometimes smell and even a visceral struggle. These factors trigger strong emotional and memory

associations that get entwined with our view of the object itself.

The IKEA effect has profound consequences and uses:

- **DIY Culture:** As we've seen, we often romanticize DIY projects, even when more effective pre-made solutions exist. The appeal lies partly in their perceived uniqueness and, crucially, the story about the effort we pour into them. This drives entire markets towards less polished but self-created items.

- **Gamification:** Many apps and programs tap into the IKEA effect by using 'quests' with small progress stages to keep users engaged. Earning badges in order to build your profile feels more special than the one-click option due to our investment of effort, however nominal.

- **Employee Motivation:** Some workplaces use collaborative build-style projects to foster feelings of shared investment and increase a sense of ownership.

- **Link to the Sunk Cost Fallacy:** While they are distinct biases, the IKEA effect can exacerbate the sunk cost fallacy. Not only have we invested money, but our labour is on the line as well – increasing our desire to stick with a suboptimal project simply due to the personal effort that's become entangled with it.

However, the IKEA effect, while undeniably impacting our decision-making, isn't inherently bad. Used wisely, it can be harnessed for good:

- **Therapeutic Applications:** Occupational therapy frequently leverages this effect, boosting patients' morale and fostering feelings of competency through hands-on projects.

- **Education:** Experiential learning taps into this effect. For instance, students who make a model volcano rather than simply watching a video retain more of their learning and gain a deeper sense of engagement with the concepts involved.

- **Relationship Building:** Parents constructing forts with their children rather than giving them a ready-made, store-bought alternative foster far more emotional connection during the process. This prioritizes time spent together rather than a perfect outcome.

Businesses have long understood the power of the IKEA effect. However, there's a thin line between clever use of customer psychology and exploitation. Here's where things get ethically troublesome:

- **Manufactured 'struggle':** Some companies design an overly difficult or convoluted product setup. This is not for functional need but to maximize the IKEA effect. Frustration undercuts any positive sense of accomplishment and damages brand loyalty over time.

- **Devaluing Expertise:** Pushing self-assembly can lead to a progressive disregard for the specialized skills of actual craftsmen. In a broader sense, this warps social understanding of labour value and promotes underpayment of workers in service-based sectors.

- **Dark Patterns in UX:** Tech companies increasingly use a deceptive gamification of the IKEA effect in app design. Time invested in trivial customization tricks users into thinking they're building something truly unique, when instead, it's primarily a tool for data acquisition and future monetization.

Questions for Self-Reflection

1. **The 'Pride Over Practicality' Trap:** When considering purchasing something you could put together yourself versus a similar yet pre-assembled item, are you honestly evaluating the trade-off between the effort involved and the quality of the final product? Or is there a bit of misplaced pride influencing your decision?

2. **Are You Gaining Mastery?** Do you recognize the difference between mastery and a mere sense of completion? When you feel a sense of accomplishment in a self-made project, is it rooted in a tangible increase in your skills or knowledge, or is it largely down to the temporary high of simply conquering a challenge? Understanding the real source of your pride helps evaluate its impact on future decisions.

3. **The Allure of Self-Made:** When choosing between experiences or items, does the effort factor distort your judgment? Are you sometimes drawn towards vacations promising hands-on involvement (building your own itinerary, etc.) over an option where experts facilitate a smoother experience, simply because the former gives an illusion of creating something unique?

4. **Gamification:** Are you aware of how gamification might be using the IKEA effect against you? Do you customize every setting on a new app for genuine usability reasons, or do meaningless badges and 'streaks' subtly increase your investment, distracting from the app's true purpose and the potential downsides of being on it?

5. **Idealising Your Effort:** At work, do you often contribute effort that doesn't fall within your core specialty? Could the IKEA effect be making you idealise the sense of 'going the extra mile' even when you are not best placed to? Does it stop you from recognizing the unique skills of colleagues that can complete the same task more quickly and effectively? This awareness is key to healthy cooperation and equitable recognition of the diverse value of various team members.

XX. THE DUNNING-KRUGER EFFECT

The Know-It-All Rookie

Alex had been at the firm less than six months, yet already his confidence radiated through the halls of the prestigious consulting agency. During project meetings, he eagerly dissected senior clients' business models, offered bold critiques of outdated practices and often hijacked presentations with his 'revolutionary' ideas. Privately, more experienced colleagues rolled their eyes. Behind his unwavering arrogance, a glaring gap revealed itself – a startling lack of understanding of the field's complexities and fundamental industry rules.

What fuelled this mismatch between Alex's perceived genius and his actual proficiency wasn't simple ego. A series of early minor wins during his onboarding had created a potent illusion. In those initial tasks, his natural quick thinking had saved the day when clients presented incomplete data sets. This instilled a belief that his intuition and ability to 'wing it' when necessary were more important than deep dives into boring industry protocols or detailed competitor analysis.

As his projects increased in scope, his facade of invincibility began to show cracks. A seasoned project manager, Amelia, witnessed his bravado crumple during a presentation where his oversimplification of the client's supply chain issues drew barely veiled contempt from industry experts on the client side. Instead of seeing this as a wake-up call, Alex doubled down, muttering about a 'generational misunderstanding' and accusing 'old-timers' of resisting innovation.

Meanwhile, the burden of cleaning up the mess his under-baked proposals caused fell increasingly on his colleagues. Resentment brewed – and worse, clients caught hints of this internal disarray through missed deadlines and inconsistent messaging. It was evident Alex's charm wouldn't be able to compensate for his deficiencies indefinitely.

The Dunning-Kruger Effect

The Dunning-Kruger effect is a nuanced psychological phenomenon that unveils the paradoxical relationship between competence and self-awareness. It delves into the cognitive bias where individuals with limited knowledge or skill in a particular domain tend to overestimate their abilities, while those with substantial expertise often underestimate theirs. This effect not only influences personal and professional growth but also impacts broader societal dynamics.

First defined by David Dunning and Justin Kruger in their seminal 1999 study, this effect highlights the metacognitive inability of individuals to recognize their lack of skill.

The Dunning-Kruger effect is primarily driven by these factors:

- **Metacognitive Deficiency:** A core issue is the individuals' inability to accurately or objectively self-assess their performance, leading to an inflated valuation. This is born of an internal illusion created by their limited experience.

- **Initial Knowledge Misinterpretation:** Early successes or the acquisition of basic knowledge can falsely signal expertise to novices. They mistake a foundational understanding for a comprehensive grasp of the subject, overlooking the depth and breadth of what they do not know.

- **Expertise Underestimation:** Conversely, highly knowledgeable individuals tend to assume that tasks that are easy for them are equally easy for others, leading them to undervalue their expertise.

The Dunning-Kruger effect has far-reaching consequences beyond individual misjudgements:

- **Professional Development and Workplace Dynamics:** It can lead to tensions in teams, misallocation of tasks and a culture that discourages feedback and learning, as individuals either overclaim expertise or fail to assert their genuine ability.

- **Financial Decision-Making:** Amateur investors or entrepreneurs may dive into complex ventures with misplaced confidence, taking financial risks based on a superficial understanding of market dynamics.

- **Public Health and Safety:** In the realm of health and safety, the effect can cause individuals to disregard expert advice in favour of simplistic solutions or conspiracy theories, undermining collective efforts to protect wellbeing.

Addressing the Dunning-Kruger effect requires targeted strategies to foster accurate self-assessment and encourage continuous learning:

- **Feedback Mechanisms:** Constructive and regular feedback can help individuals calibrate their self-assessments with external evaluations.

- **Lifelong Learning:** Cultivating an environment that values continuous education and skill development can mitigate overconfidence in novices and encourage experts to value and share their knowledge.

- **Metacognitive Skills:** Teaching metacognitive strategies can help individuals become more aware of their learning processes, strengths and weaknesses, fostering a more accurate understanding of their abilities.

The Dunning-Kruger effect underscores the intricate relationship between knowledge, self-perception and cognitive bias. By recognizing the manifestations and implications of this effect, individuals and organizations can implement strategies to promote a culture of humility, lifelong learning and accurate self-reflection. This not only enhances personal and professional growth but also contributes to the development of a more informed, open-minded and competent society.

Questions for Self-Reflection

1. **Openness to Criticism:** Are you open to feedback? Can you accept constructive criticism without defensiveness? Truly competent people want to improve and not just protect their egos.

2. **Accepting Your Limits:** Can you say 'I don't know'? Being comfortable with uncertainty is a sign of maturity. It's also the first step towards seeking out the knowledge we lack.

3. **Valuing Others:** Do you value the expertise of others? Do you respect what experts know, even when it challenges your own views? Do you avoid the temptation to dismiss views that contradict your current understanding of a topic?

4. **Putting in the Work:** Are you willing to put in the work? True competence isn't achieved through initial bursts of confidence. It requires the sustained effort of learning and practice.

5. **Superficiality vs Depth:** Do you confuse strong opinions with deep understanding? In a world saturated with information, it's easy to form quick, confident opinions on complex subjects. Are we willing to challenge these opinions, dig deeper and consider alternative perspectives?

XXI. NEGATIVITY BIAS

The World Through Smoke-Coloured Glasses

Sarah's approach to life, marked by a blend of realism and inherent scepticism, had long been her armour against the world's unpredictability. This shield, she believed, fortified her against disappointments and softened the blow of life's myriad letdowns. It was a strategy born of experience; a method to temper expectations and find delight in life's unexpected joys. Yet, what once felt like prudence began to morph into a pervasive gloom, colouring her view of the world in stark shades of grey.

Each morning, her journey to work was carried out in silent contemplation. The bustling city, alive with the rhythm of countless stories, appeared to Sarah as a tableau of frustration and decay. Where some saw the convenience of urban life, she noticed only its failings – the litter that clung to the pavements like autumn leaves, the weary expressions of morning commuters and the unsettling vibrations of the train that seemed to whisper warnings to her. These observations, though rooted in reality, were filtered through a lens that magnified every flaw, casting a pall over the vibrant life around her.

At her job, this tendency to spotlight problems infiltrated her professional interactions and self-perception. Feedback, however constructive, felt like a harbinger of future failure, a sign that her efforts were not only unappreciated but also inadequate. Mistakes, no matter how minor, were inflated into glaring evidence of incompetence, not just in others but in herself too. This constant focus on the negative began to erode her confidence and sense of belonging, transforming her workplace into a place of fear and potential failure rather than opportunities for growth and achievement.

This habit extended its reach into her personal life, colouring interactions and straining relationships with friends and family. Conversations were navigated like minefields, with Sarah on alert for any hint of criticism or disappointment. Social gatherings, once a source of joy, became exercises in endurance as she braced for the inevitable letdowns and misunderstandings.

As the weight of this negativity grew heavier, Sarah began to recognize the toll it was taking on her wellbeing. The realization that her scepticism had spiralled into a pervasive sense of pessimism prompted a moment of introspection. Was her cautious approach to life actually a barrier to experiencing its full richness and complexity? The acknowledgment of this pattern was the first step towards change.

Determined to shift her perspective, Sarah embarked on a journey of self-discovery and transformation. She sought out practices that encouraged mindfulness and gratitude, focusing on the present moment and acknowledging the positives that had always existed alongside the negatives. She challenged herself to find beauty in the mundane, to appreciate the small victories at work and to embrace the imperfections in herself and others with empathy and understanding.

This deliberate shift in focus was not an overnight transformation but a gradual reorientation of her outlook on life. Sarah discovered that by acknowledging the negatives without allowing them to dominate her perspective, she could enjoy a more balanced and fulfilling experience of the world and an appreciation of life's complexities. The journey was challenging, yet it offered Sarah a newfound sense of peace and contentment. She learned that a healthy dose of scepticism could coexist with an open heart and a hopeful spirit.

Negativity Bias

Negativity bias, a pervasive aspect of human psychology, explains the disproportionate weight we place on negative aspects of our experiences. This bias shapes how we interpret and interact with the world, impacting us in many different ways, from decision-making and risk assessment to our interpersonal relationships and wellbeing.

Negativity bias can be traced back to our primal survival mechanisms. For early humans, quickly recognizing and reacting to potential threats (such as predators or natural hazards) was crucial for survival. This resulted in a brain that is more attuned to negative information, as failing to notice a threat could have fatal consequences. While modern humans rarely face such immediate threats, the underlying psychological bias remains, influencing our behaviour in less life-threatening contexts. These powerful evolutionary roots are what make it such a complex problem to resolve.

Several psychological mechanisms contribute to negativity bias:

- **Memory and Recall:** Negative experiences are often remembered more vividly and for longer periods than positive ones. This can colour our overall memories and perceptions of past events, leading to a skewed perspective.

- **Attention and Perception:** Individuals tend to pay more attention to negative information, whether it's news stories, critical feedback or potential risks. This heightened attention can disproportionately influence our judgments and decisions.

- **Emotional Impact:** Negative emotions generally involve more thinking and information processing than positive ones. They also prompt more rumination, further reinforcing their impact on our psyche.

The effects of negativity bias extend beyond individual cognition, influencing societal norms and personal wellbeing:

- **Media Consumption:** The old adage, 'If it bleeds, it leads', reflects negativity bias in media consumption. News outlets and social media platforms often emphasize negative stories as they attract more attention, leading to a distorted perception of reality.

- **Risk Aversion:** In decision-making, negativity bias can lead to excessive risk aversion. Individuals may focus more on potential losses than on equivalent gains, which can impact everything from financial investments to personal growth opportunities.

- **Interpersonal Dynamics:** Negativity bias can strain relationships, as individuals may fixate on their partners' flaws or interpret ambiguous comments negatively.

Addressing negativity bias involves conscious effort and strategies to recalibrate our perceptions:

- **Mindfulness and Positive Reframing:** Practicing mindfulness can help individuals become more aware of their tendency to focus on the negative, allowing for intentional shifts towards positive reframing.

- **Gratitude Practices:** Regularly identifying and reflecting on positive aspects of one's life can counterbalance negativity bias, enhancing overall wellbeing.

- **Diversified Information Sources:** Actively seeking out positive news and limiting exposure to sensationalist media can help mitigate the impact of negativity bias on your worldview.

- **Cognitive-Behavioural Strategies:** Techniques such as cognitive restructuring can help individuals challenge and change negative thought patterns, promoting a more balanced perspective.

Negativity bias, while rooted in evolutionary survival mechanisms, exerts a profound influence on modern human behaviour, affecting everything from our daily mood to political manoeuvring. By understanding and actively addressing this bias, individuals can foster more balanced perceptions, healthier relationships and greater resilience.

Questions for Self-Reflection

Do you see Sarah's struggle mirrored, even to a small degree, in your own outlook? Consider these questions:

1. **Mental Spotlight:** During your day, where does your attention naturally gravitate? Do negative news stories feel more important than positive ones?

2. **One Bad Apple:** Can a single critical comment overshadow numerous compliments? Do minor mishaps linger in your mind far longer than successes?

3. **What If?** Does anticipating problems fill your mental space? Do you spend more time planning for negatives than savouring what goes right?

4. **Are You a Flaw Finder?** Does your inner dialogue highlight what's wrong or unfair in relationships and situations more often than noting the good?

5. **Recalling the Bad:** When reflecting on your past, do negative memories stand out with greater clarity and significance than positive ones?

XXII. THE JUST-WORLD FALLACY

The Search for Meaning

Lily was raised with a strong sense of right and wrong. Hard work equalled success; poor behaviour eventually reaped negative consequences. She believed there was a fundamental fairness woven into the universe; a force that rewarded virtue and punished wrongdoing. But then, life handed her a blow that challenged these deep-rooted beliefs to the core.

Her husband, Mark, the picture of health and good habits, was diagnosed with an aggressive form of cancer. It felt like a cosmic betrayal. He'd followed the rules – never smoking, eating well and maintaining an active lifestyle. In those sleepless nights on the uncomfortable hospital couch, Lily wrestled with an insidious guilt. Had she missed something? Did some hidden fault warrant such pain? This wasn't how the world was supposed to work.

As Mark slipped away, an uncomfortable realization surfaced alongside Lily's profound grief. Her usual circle of friends, once a source of solace, offered platitudes that grated against her raw heart. 'He's in a better place now', or 'Everything happens for a reason', echoed hollowly. Even those who gave her genuine sympathy spoke to her with this unnerving undercurrent. There was a quiet implication that if there was meaning in Mark's death, then perhaps every life, however well-lived, carried the hidden seeds of tragedy.

At first, she blamed this existential discomfort on her grief warping the good intentions of those around her. Yet, something more troubling lingered in her thoughts. In the quiet hours, alone with her memories and fears, a voice whispered: if good lives weren't exempt from suffering, did that mean her own happiness was built on quicksand? Maybe she didn't truly deserve her successes – they could be snatched away as arbitrarily as Mark's health. This realization felt more ominous than grief itself.

The Just-World Fallacy

This psychological pitfall has a name: the just-world fallacy. It's the widely held, yet fundamentally flawed, belief that the world is inherently fair and that our actions always have morally congruent consequences – 'good' results will appear from 'good' deeds, and 'bad' outcomes stem from 'bad' choices. It's an alluring concept, especially for those of us with a strong moral compass and a drive to exert control over life's chaos.

The need for justice runs deep within human psychology. From early childhood, we develop expectations about fair treatment. For the most part, this sense serves us well, promoting fairness and accountability within society. However, when stretched to breaking point, this desire for inherent order in the world can backfire with unintended consequences:

- **The Illusion of Control:** The belief in a just world reinforces the idea that we have agency over our lives. This offers a comforting feeling of protection: 'As long as I don't mess up, bad things won't happen'. But this is ultimately false and a precarious position to put ourselves in.

- **Self-Righteousness:** The flipside of the just-world belief is a tendency to find fault with ourselves or others when misfortune strikes. This allows us to maintain the just-world belief, but it ignores the chaotic, unjust randomness in life.

- **Victim Blaming:** Clinging to this fallacy often involves making assumptions about those who are suffering to preserve our sense of fairness in the world. For instance, it might manifest itself in judgement of others' circumstances: 'They must have brought it on themselves', 'If they tried harder, they wouldn't be in this situation', and, 'That would never happen to me'. This belief that individuals bring their own suffering upon themselves encourages judgement and erodes compassion. It also provides a scapegoat for the real cause of problems, preventing the search for a solution. This attitude can appear within both large-scale narratives (blaming communities for their poverty and neglecting systemic solutions) and within our daily interactions (assuming a laid-off friend must have had a poor work ethic and not giving them support).

- **Romanticizing Suffering:** The belief that hardships build character (that hard work brings good tidings) can degrade into dismissing genuine pain from illness or discrimination as somehow necessary for 'growth'.

- **Superstitious 'Karmic' Thinking:** Viewing setbacks as punishment for past, unrelated flaws or mistakes makes every struggle about our own moral failing instead of external forces or just the complex randomness of life.

- **The Trauma of Realization:** If our just-world belief is shaken, as it was with Lily, it may traumatise us and lead us to overcorrect. If tragedy can strike out of nowhere, what's the point in being good or putting in effort? The realization that we have no control creates extreme vulnerability to what is unrelenting uncertainty.

In the aftermath of Mark's death, Lily grappled with the dissonance created by the just-world fallacy. Intellectually, she recognized the illogic behind the nagging fears that she might somehow be culpable for her husband's death. Decades of personal experience reinforced her understanding of how disease worked. Logically, she accepted his illness was not a punishment, not a tool to balance the cosmic scales of good and evil. On a conscious level, she rejected victim-blaming attitudes.

Yet, emotionally, that need for fairness still resonated. As much as she hated admitting it, a tiny shard of doubt remained. She began noticing those thoughts with brutal honesty, recognizing how the same bias subtly permeated her views on subjects less personally devastating. In a new story about rising homelessness, didn't a hint of self-righteousness arise while thinking, 'I work hard, so why don't they?' At times, she caught herself dismissing a colleague's professional troubles, almost subconsciously, with the notion that some unidentified character flaw must be to blame. These thoughts brought her shame, yet the bias proved difficult to fully erase.

The allure of just-world beliefs isn't a sign of cruelty or ignorance. It's a powerful psychological coping mechanism. Facing life's inherent injustice feels unbearable, so finding an explanation is a protective tactic to retain a sense of hope and meaning. In a world of senseless tragedy, victim blaming allows people to believe that they themselves are immune because they somehow play by different rules.

This fallacy offers the illusion of predictability – do 'x' and you can expect 'y'. It's reassuring to believe we understand how things work, when often, in reality, we are operating in chaos disguised as order. The problem surfaces when those explanations distort our empathy and our belief in an ordered world blinds us to systemic issues (poverty and healthcare inequities, for example). This is when blame gets deflected towards easy, and often incorrect, targets.

Questions for Self-Reflection

Lily's experience is a wake-up call. We all fall prey to just-world thinking to some degree. Examining its influence involves taking off the rose-tinted glasses and asking ourselves tough questions:

1. **Making Assumptions:** How does your need for fairness shape reality? Are you quick to attribute another's suffering to specific 'wrongdoings' before searching for broader causes?

2. **In the Driving Seat:** Are you too optimistic about your own level of control? Where do you draw the line between taking responsibility for improvement and assuming you're immune to unfair outcomes simply because of 'good' life choices?

3. **Secret Judgments:** When hearing of another's struggles, do hidden thoughts arise in you around them inviting that

situation? Are those assumptions challenged upon introspection?

4. **Qualified Compassion:** Are you guilty of offering empathy that always includes a qualification about how a situation is at least partially someone's own fault?

5. **Ignoring Systemic Problems:** Does a focus on individual responsibility for misfortunes prevent you from critically examining underlying social, economic or political injustices?

XXIII. THE FALSE CONSENSUS EFFECT

The Invisible Consensus

Emily was beyond frustrated. After the contentious town hall meeting on the proposed park development, it seemed like the whole town was against her. Didn't they see what she saw? The crumbling playgrounds, the lack of safe spaces for kids and the obvious benefit a vibrant park would offer the whole community. To her, it was clear as day – a slam dunk of an idea. Yet, resistance and hostility had been pervasive in the meeting.

Intrigued by the fierce counter-arguments, Emily started conversations with various neighbours to try and understand why they were so vehemently opposed to what she felt was a universally positive development. To her surprise, a pattern emerged. Many who shared her general desire for improvements in their community weren't on board with *this* park. Concerns ranged from worries about increased traffic, suspicion of hidden tax increases or simply desiring a different kind of amenity.

Her bubble of assumed agreement burst; Emily was shocked. Was this how most people in town felt?

The False Consensus Effect

Emily had fallen victim to the false consensus effect. This powerful cognitive bias leads us to instinctively overestimate the degree to which others share our beliefs, opinions and preferences. We are naturally prone to projecting our own worldviews onto others, assuming they see things the same way we do.

Here are some questions to help us understand this phenomenon and its impact on us in all sorts of situations:

- **The Exposure Question:** When we surround ourselves with like-minded people, or predominantly consume information that aligns with our own views, are we getting a truly representative sample of other perspectives?

- **The Evidence Question:** Are we always operating on solid evidence of agreement, or are we basing our assessment of what others believe primarily on assumptions and intuition?

- **The Blind Spot Question:** Even when we have genuine empathy, can we truly know how another might feel or the exact motivations behind their opinions without direct understanding of their experiences?

The false consensus effect, while pervasive, isn't something we're entirely powerless against. Emily began breaking through her echo chamber and understanding the nuanced viewpoints of the townspeople through respectful conversation. Let's consider ways to mitigate this bias in our own lives:

- **Active Listening:** Seek to truly understand and hear perspectives that differ from your own. Be mindful of simply waiting for your turn to speak or formulating counter-arguments – focus on genuinely hearing the other person out.

- **Exposure to Diversity:** Intentionally broaden your social and informational circles. Engaging with a wide variety of opinions challenges your assumptions and provides a realistic snapshot of the full spectrum of human thought.

- **The Value of Doubt:** Approach situations, particularly emotionally charged ones, with a healthy dose of scepticism towards your own certainty. Acknowledge that differing opinions might be well-founded and worth investigating.

Emily realized that she'd misjudged the scope of support for the park project based on her own enthusiasm and belief in its merit. Instead of assuming consensus, she opened herself to dialogue and discovered that others, while sharing her desire for a better community, had valid reasons for wanting different outcomes. It was a powerful lesson in not mistaking her own perspective for a universal truth.

The false consensus effect is our constant companion, subtly colouring our thoughts, feelings and decision-making. By developing an awareness of it, seeking diverse opinions, asking ourselves tough questions and cultivating a practice of empathy, we can mitigate its influence and create a more open-minded and understanding approach to the world around us.

Initially, Emily felt slightly deflated about having her assumptions challenged. The illusion of widespread support had fuelled her mission. However, as she continued to engage in open conversations and let her curiosity lead her, a new path emerged. This time, instead of pushing an outcome that aligned with *her* ideal, she actively invited everyone to participate.

Emily hosted smaller gatherings, ensuring varied perspectives had a seat at the table. Together, they delved into the concerns and hopes held by both the pro-park and anti-park camps. Surprisingly, a significant amount of common ground began to surface. Everyone craved a vibrant community space and was invested in the wellbeing of their families. From there, conversations bloomed with a new energy.

As a result, compromise arose. The new park was scaled down to address traffic concerns and included elements that appeased those initially in opposition. A walking trail satisfied nature lovers, and a new playscape became the crown jewel of their plan, thrilling parents and children alike. Had Emily remained rooted in her initial belief in consensus without actively investigating other perspectives, this outcome might never have emerged.

The experience sparked a change in Emily, not just on that specific project, but in her approach to the community as a whole.

- **'Obvious' Isn't Always So:** When new issues, proposals or points of debate arose, Emily no longer fell into her well-worn mental groove of believing, 'Surely, everyone sees it my way'. A more questioning mindset gave her greater understanding and patience in all kinds of discussions.

- **Humility Takes the Stage:** Realizing the limits of her own perspective had a humbling effect. She listened more, asserted less and began to see her own convictions as just one set of beliefs among many. This made her an effective mediator and negotiator in other town committees she joined.

- **Empathy as a Bridge:** As assumptions were replaced with understanding, Emily began to see the 'opposition' not as adversaries but as people equally concerned about the town's wellbeing. They just had different approaches to tackling shared problems. This shift from an 'us vs them' mentality created fertile ground for building connection and trust.

Questions for Self-Reflection

Emily's story highlights some ways questioning perceived consensus can be transformative.

1. **Your Opinion Ecosystem:** Where do you get most of your information and spend your social time? Does this present a balanced picture of reality, or are you in an echo chamber of opinions similar to your own?

2. **Challenge Your Convictions:** How often do you genuinely put yourself in the shoes of those who see things differently? Where might your biases and assumptions be limiting your understanding?

3. **From Opinion to Dialogue:** Instead of starting conversations convinced of your own rightness, can you approach opposing views as an opportunity for growth and a broadening of perspective?

4. **The Blind Spots of Success:** Consider a success you've had, particularly one achieved through teamwork or collaboration. Did you fully grasp the unique contributions and perspectives

of others on the team, or did you assume everyone approached the problem like you did?

5. **Navigating Conflict:** We are constantly exposed to conflicts, large and small, whether social issues, family disagreements or clashes of opinion in the workplace. How might stepping back and asking, 'Am I falling prey to the false consensus effect here?' allow you to navigate these situations more productively?

XXIV. THE PLACEBO EFFECT

The Enigma of the Placebo

Sarah's battle with insomnia had become an all-consuming struggle, transforming night after night into a prolonged ordeal of restlessness and frustration. The quest for a peaceful night's sleep seemed endless, with each tick of the clock marking another lost opportunity. Traditional remedies and over-the-counter sleep aids offered little relief, often leaving her feeling more exhausted and disoriented the next day than if she had not slept at all. Desperate for a solution, Sarah turned to the promise of modern medicine, volunteering to participate in a clinical trial for an innovative new drug touted as a breakthrough in the treatment of insomnia.

With a mixture of hope and lingering scepticism, Sarah embarked on the trial, diligently adhering to the regimen prescribed by the research team. As the weeks progressed, she began to notice a significant shift in her sleeping patterns. The hours spent tossing and turning diminished, replaced by a newfound ability to drift off with ease. Mornings arrived with a sense of rejuvenation she hadn't felt in months, if not years. The transformation was remarkable.

However, during a routine check-in with the research team, Sarah was confronted with a revelation that completely upended her understanding of her recent improvement. The lead researcher, reviewing her file with clinical detachment, informed her that she had been part of the control group throughout the trial. The pills she had been taking were nothing more than sugar pills, devoid of any medicinal properties – a placebo.

The news sent Sarah reeling, her mind grappling with the implications of what she had just learned. The very foundation of her recovery, which she had attributed to the cutting-edge medication, was revealed to be a construct of her own mind driven by her belief in the treatment. The realization that she could conjure such a profound physical response to a substance with no inherent therapeutic value was both shocking and enlightening.

As Sarah reflected on her experience, she began to explore the power of the placebo effect – the phenomenon by which a patient's symptoms can be alleviated simply because the individual believes in their treatment's efficacy. This unexpected journey into the realm of psychosomatic healing prompted Sarah to reconsider the interplay between mind and body and between belief, expectation and physical health.

The revelation that her improvement was self-induced sparked a curiosity in Sarah about our capacity for self-healing and the role of mental state in physical wellbeing. It opened her eyes to the untapped potential within her to influence her own health outcomes by harnessing this effect, not as a substitute for medical treatment but as a complementary force. She was left with a new understanding of the power of belief and the untold capabilities of the human mind.

The Placebo Effect

The placebo effect demonstrates the remarkable power of the mind over the body. A placebo is a substance or treatment without any therapeutic ingredients, designed to resemble actual medical treatment. As we saw above, people sometimes experience real changes in their symptoms when receiving a placebo. It can lead to positive effects such as pain reduction, mood elevation and improved symptoms in a variety of conditions, including the following:

- Depression
- Anxiety
- Irritable bowel syndrome (IBS)
- Insomnia
- Parkinson's disease

While the exact mechanisms behind the placebo effect remain somewhat mysterious, researchers have identified several key factors that play a role:

- **Expectation:** Belief in the effectiveness of a treatment is potent. If we expect something to make us feel better, our brains release chemicals like endorphins (natural painkillers) and dopamine (a neurotransmitter tied to reward), mirroring the actual physiological response of medication.

- **Classical Conditioning:** Think of Pavlov's famous dogs – after repeatedly pairing food (stimulus) with a bell (neutral stimulus), the dogs began salivating (response) with the bell alone. In a similar vein, our bodies sometimes become conditioned. If we've felt pain relief following a medical procedure in the past, the setting, ritual and even the appearance of similar treatments can trigger an improvement in symptoms, regardless of the actual treatment received.

- **Provider-Patient Relationship:** A genuine, positive doctor-patient dynamic boosts a patient's sense of trust and optimism, enhancing the placebo effect. This highlights why bedside manner and genuine care contribute significantly to healing outcomes.

- **Mind-Body Connection:** Our thoughts, emotions and stress levels exert a profound influence over our physiology. The placebo effect sheds light on how positive expectations and a hopeful outlook can activate pathways within the body that support self-healing.

While largely beneficial, the placebo effect raises ethical questions. Is it ever justified to utilize placebos in a patient's treatment if it might help? While this debate carries no simple answer, here are some points to ponder:

- **Informed Consent:** In research studies, participants are thoroughly informed about the potential inclusion of placebos. In everyday medical practice, however, the line blurs –should a doctor prescribe a placebo – such as a non-essential vitamin – if the patient believes that it's actually a powerful medicine? If they told them the truth, however, it would undermine the placebo effect.

- **Temporary Gains:** Sometimes, a placebo effect may offer temporary relief but fail to address the underlying cause of an illness. Relying only on a placebo, especially in the case of serious conditions, poses inherent risks.

- **The Power of Suggestion:** Placebos highlight potential flaws in relying solely on self-reported improvements. Could the desire to please a doctor or researcher skew how a patient rates their progress?

The influence of our expectations and mental outlook isn't only restricted to medical treatment. Consider these other ways in which the placebo effect touches our lives:

- **Supplements and Wellness Practices:** From dietary aids with exaggerated claims to trendy detox rituals, the allure of quick fixes and promised cures capitalizes on a psychological placebo effect.

- **Performance Enhancement Supplements:** The ritual of taking a pre-workout supplement to 'boost' our performance might have less to do with the ingredients and more to do with the athlete's primed psychological state and confidence.

- **Everyday 'Cures':** Think of your favourite home remedy for the common cold, perhaps passed down through generations. Some of its effectiveness might lie in the ritual itself, the feeling of care it promotes and the positive associations around it.

The mind-body connection illustrated by the placebo effect hints at an undeniable truth: our beliefs and attitudes are more potent than we sometimes realize. This awareness grants us a level of personal power and choice in managing our own wellbeing. Instead of seeing health purely as the work of medications and external procedures, we can harness the potential within. Let's consider some approaches that help us do this:

- **The Practice of Optimism:** A positive outlook not only enhances happiness but has implications for physical wellbeing. While this doesn't negate the need for appropriate medical attention, fostering an optimistic mindset can bolster traditional treatment approaches.

- **Cultivating Healthy Rituals:** Whether it's a simple mindfulness meditation before bed, a favourite herbal tea for calm or setting aside time for a relaxing bath, building rituals centred around our personal sense of wellbeing taps into the placebo effect's underlying principle.

- **Mindful Scepticism:** Understanding how easily belief can cloud perception arms us with critical thinking tools. As we encounter new health trends, miracle cures and bold promises in the wellness arena, a dose of healthy scepticism encourages us to dig for reliable information and not rely solely on anecdotal evidence.

Questions for Self-Reflection

The placebo effect raises fascinating questions about personal beliefs, habits and how we approach our physical and mental health.

1. **Identifying Your Rituals:** Do you have habits or rituals that support your sense of wellbeing? Can you recognize a

component of positive expectation that might bolster their effectiveness?

2. **Challenging Self-Doubt:** Does a negative narrative sometimes play into your perception of symptoms or treatment? Do phrases like, 'This will never work', or 'I'll never feel better', create a counterproductive cycle? Can you practice reframing those thoughts into ones of possibility?

3. **The Role of the Provider:** Consider your interactions with healthcare professionals. Do you feel a sense of trust and open communication, or is there a feeling of detachment that may diminish your belief in treatments?

4. **Fact vs Belief in Wellness Trends:** Before committing to a new diet, supplement or treatment, consider your process for verifying its claims. Do you carry out some independent research? Is there a balance between personal testimonials and hard data?

5. **Placebos and Personal Responsibility:** Does learning about the placebo effect make you feel empowered or perhaps discouraged? Is there a need to reevaluate the role of active management vs reliance on a 'quick fix' for health concerns?

XXV. MENTAL ACCOUNTING

The Sacred Pot of Savings

Elena, with her disciplined approach to personal finance, had always been the epitome of fiscal responsibility among her circle of friends and family. Her knack for budgeting and making astute investment choices was not just a matter of pride but a testament to her deep understanding of financial planning. Over time, Elena had developed a robust system for managing her finances, dividing her income into meticulously categorized accounts: a savings account earmarked for emergencies, a checking account dedicated to handling daily expenditures and various investment portfolios designed to secure her retirement and fund her children's education. Each account had its specific role, forming an integral part of Elena's carefully constructed financial strategy.

This harmonious system was put to the test when Elena was suddenly faced with an unforeseen challenge – a hefty medical bill that demanded immediate payment. This financial strain coincided with a downturn in the market, which had adversely affected the value of her investment portfolio. Despite the fact she had sufficient funds in her savings account to cover the expense, Elena found herself reluctant to tap into it. In her mind, this was a sacrosanct reserve, to be breached only in the most critical of emergencies. The idea of using these funds for her current predicament seemed incongruent with the purpose she had assigned to it.

Elena contemplated liquidating a portion of her investment portfolio to settle the bill, even though it meant realizing a loss given the current market conditions. This course of action baffled her loved ones, who viewed the well-funded savings account as the clear solution to her dilemma. However, Elena's thinking was clouded by the mental barriers she had erected around her finances. The rigid compartments into which she had organized her money – each with its designated use – created a psychological obstacle that made the straightforward act of using her savings for an unexpected bill feel like a breach of her financial principles.

Elena's predicament highlights the powerful influence of mental accounting, a cognitive bias where individuals categorize, prioritize and treat money differently based on subjective criteria, often leading to irrational financial decisions. This bias had led Elena to a crossroads, forcing her to weigh the perceived sanctity of her savings against the practicality of addressing her immediate financial needs without incurring unnecessary losses. The struggle between adhering to her self-imposed financial rules and responding pragmatically to an unexpected expense underscored the complex interplay between psychological biases and personal finance management.

Mental Accounting

Mental accounting is a concept rooted in behavioural economics. It explains how individuals classify, evaluate and manage their finances through psychological categorization. This theory, pioneered by Richard Thaler, posits that people don't treat money as fungible – interchangeable and indistinct – but rather assign it to different 'accounts' or 'funds' based on various subjective criteria such as the source of the money, its intended use or the timing of the expenditure.

Mental accounting operates on several key principles that affect financial decision-making:

- **Source Dependence:** The origin of money influences how it is spent or saved. For example, individuals may splurge with a windfall – like a tax refund or a lottery win – much more readily than they would with their regular income, perceiving it as 'bonus' or 'extra' money, even though all money is inherently interchangeable.

- **Transaction Utility:** This principle suggests that people derive satisfaction or pain not just from the outcome of a financial decision but also from the perceived value of the transaction itself. For instance, buying an item on sale provides a sense of gain beyond the actual saving, influencing spending behaviour.

- **Intended Use:** Funds earmarked for specific purposes (e.g., vacation, education, retirement) are less likely to be reallocated, even when it might be financially prudent to do so. This segmentation can lead to illogical financial practices, such as carrying high-interest credit card debt while holding money in low-interest savings accounts earmarked for another purpose.

Mental accounting has profound behavioural implications, influencing how individuals save, spend, invest and perceive value:

- **Spending Behaviour:** The classification of money into different mental accounts can lead to asymmetric spending behaviours. For instance, individuals may be more willing to spend money classified as 'disposable income' on non-essential items than they would be to dip into savings for the same purchase.

- **Investment Decisions:** Investors might treat dividends differently from capital gains, despite their economic equivalence, leading to suboptimal investment strategies. For example, an investor might reinvest dividends but be reluctant to sell shares to realize a capital gain.

- **Saving and Borrowing:** Mental accounting can result in seemingly paradoxical situations, such as individuals saving for a future goal at a low interest rate while maintaining high-interest debt. The separation between 'debt' and 'savings' in their mental accounting leads to a disregard for the overall financial picture.

While mental accounting provides insightful explanations for many irrational financial behaviours, it has faced criticism as a concept, primarily for its descriptive rather than predictive nature. Critics argue that it cannot reliably predict how individuals will categorize and perceive different financial scenarios, so it cannot be utilized effectively to prevent problems occurring.

However, some argue that understanding the concept of mental accounting is crucial for designing better financial products, advising strategies and personal financial planning. Recognizing people's natural tendencies to mentally categorize money can lead to more effective saving, spending and investing habits.

Acknowledging the influence of mental accounting is the first step towards mitigating its potentially negative impacts. Individuals can adopt several strategies to counteract mental accounting biases:

- **Holistic Financial Planning:** Viewing finances comprehensively rather than as segregated accounts can help in making decisions that optimize overall financial health.

- **Flexibility in Financial Goals:** While earmarking funds for specific purposes can be motivational, maintaining flexibility allows for the reallocation of resources as priorities and circumstances change, optimizing your financial outcomes.

- **Education and Awareness:** Understanding the principles of mental accounting and recognizing its influence on personal financial decisions can empower individuals to make more rational and less emotionally driven choices.

Mental accounting is a testament to the complexity of human cognition and its profound impact on financial behaviour. By dissecting its mechanisms and implications, individuals can better navigate the psychological underpinnings of their financial decisions, leading to improved financial wellbeing and investment success.

Questions for Self-Reflection

1. **Categorization:** Reflect on how you categorize your finances. Have you ever treated money differently based on its source or

intended use? How might this have influenced your spending or saving decisions?

2. **Choosing What's Optimal:** Consider a time when you faced a financial decision involving different 'accounts'. Did you choose the option that was financially optimal, or were your decisions influenced by the mental accounts you had set up?

3. **Found Money:** Think about any 'found' money you've received, such as tax refunds, bonuses or gifts. How did you decide to use this money? Did you perceive and use it differently than your regular income?

4. **Savings and Debt:** Reflect on your savings and debt. Have you ever kept savings intact while carrying debt, even when the debt had a higher interest rate than the return on your savings? What motivated this choice?

5. **Safeguards:** Evaluate your approach to financial decision-making. How can understanding mental accounting help you make more rational financial decisions? What steps can you take to minimize its negative impacts?

XXVI. THE CURSE OF KNOWLEDGE

The Expert's Dilemma

Dr. Emily Chen, a vanguard in the field of biotechnology, stood at the forefront of a scientific revolution. Her groundbreaking research promised a new dawn in the treatment of a rare genetic disorder that had eluded the grasp of medical science for decades. The potential of her work had not only captivated her peers but also drawn the keen interest of investors looking for the next big leap in medical technology. It had also attracted the media, eager to report on what could be a milestone achievement in science.

Emily's journey began with a presentation to her fellow scientists at a prestigious conference. Armed with data, graphs and the intricate details of her research, she delved into the nuances of her work, expecting a high level of technical understanding. Her expectations became reality; her audience were captivated, their enthusiasm palpable, and their questions reflected a deep engagement and genuine interest. This initial success buoyed her spirits, reinforcing her belief in the transformative potential of her research.

Riding the wave of this early success, Emily prepared for her next challenge: presenting her research to potential investors. Unlike her scientific audience, these were businessmen and women with a keen eye for potential but not necessarily a background in biotechnology. Emily, confident in the substance of her work, approached this presentation with the same level of detail and technical depth as she had with her scientific peers. However, the complexity of her research, so fascinating to scientists, proved to be a barrier for the investors. Their faces, a mix of confusion and polite interest, reflected a disconnect. Questions went unanswered, not for lack of effort on Emily's part, but due to a fundamental gap in their understanding. The investors, overwhelmed by the technical jargon and intricate data, found it difficult to see the forest for the trees and failed to appreciate the groundbreaking potential of Emily's research.

This disconnect became even more pronounced when Emily attempted to convey the significance of her work to the media. A journalist, intrigued by the buzz surrounding Emily's research, sought to capture its essence for the broader public. However, the complexity of the subject matter proved to be a stumbling block. The resulting article, intending to demystify her work, instead muddled the facts, presenting a distorted view, rife with inaccuracies and misunderstandings.

This series of miscommunications served as a pivotal moment for Emily. She realized that her deep immersion in her field had inadvertently created a language barrier between her and those outside her immediate circle of scientific peers. The challenge was no longer just about advancing her research but about bridging the gap between her ability to communicate this opportunity and the understanding of the general public, investors and media.

Determined to overcome this obstacle, Emily embarked on a journey to refine her communication skills. She sought advice from colleagues, attended workshops and practiced simplifying her explanations without diluting the essence of her research. Her efforts were aimed not just at sharing her knowledge but at fostering a genuine understanding and appreciation of her work's potential impact on the world.

As Emily honed her ability to communicate complex ideas in an accessible manner, she not only paved the way for her research to receive the recognition and support it deserved but also highlighted the importance of clear communication in the pursuit of scientific advancement. Her story serves as a testament to the idea that breakthroughs in science not only require innovation and dedication but also the ability to share one's vision with the world.

The Curse of Knowledge

The 'curse of knowledge' is a cognitive bias that occurs when an individual, possessing a certain level of expertise or knowledge about a subject, finds it difficult to think about that subject from the perspective of someone with less knowledge. This bias can lead to communication challenges, as experts may assume that their audience has a similar background, uses the same terminology or holds the same assumptions.

The concept was first identified by economists Colin Camerer, George Loewenstein and Martin Weber in 1989, who observed that better-informed economic entities were unable to ignore the private knowledge they possessed when predicting others' decisions. This bias stems from the difficulty of undoing or suppressing one's own knowledge to simulate a less informed perspective.

The curse of knowledge has significant implications in education, business, marketing and in any field where information is shared between parties of differing levels of understanding. For example, educators might struggle to teach basic concepts that they find intuitively obvious, while entrepreneurs might fail to convey the value of their products to consumers or investors.

To mitigate the effects of the curse of knowledge, individuals can use the following:

- **Employ Analogies and Simplifications:** Using relatable analogies can help bridge the gap between complex concepts and the audience's understanding.

- **Seek Feedback from Diverse Audiences:** Regularly testing one's explanations on people with varying levels of knowledge can highlight areas of confusion.

- **Practice Empathy:** Actively trying to adopt the perspective of one's audience can guide the simplification process and make communication more effective.

Questions for Self-Reflection

1. **Making Assumptions:** Reflect on a situation where you struggled to explain a concept you're familiar with to someone with less knowledge. What assumptions did you make about their level of understanding?

2. **Experiencing the Curse of Knowledge:** Consider a time when you were on the receiving end of the curse of knowledge. How did it affect your ability to understand the information being presented?

3. **Effective Techniques:** Think about the techniques you've used to simplify complex information. Which were most effective and why?

4. **Learning from Non-Expert Feedback:** Recall an instance where feedback from a non-expert helped you improve your communication. What did you learn from that experience?

5. **Refining Communication Strategies:** Evaluate your current communication strategies. How can you apply insights from understanding the curse of knowledge to be more effective in sharing information with diverse audiences?

XXVII. THE SOCRATIC PARADOX

The Wisdom of Uncertainty

Sarah Jennings stood at the zenith of the tech world, her name synonymous with visionary leadership and groundbreaking innovations. For years, her insights had steered her company through the tempestuous seas of the industry, guiding it past shoals of obsolescence into the open waters of market dominance. Yet, on the eve of a distinguished leadership seminar, Sarah found herself grappling with the essence of her own wisdom. It was a moment of introspection that would illuminate the depths of her understanding and redefine her approach to decision-making.

The seminar provided Sarah with a stage not just to impart knowledge but to delve into the intricacies of leadership in an ever-evolving industry. Her audience, a collection of aspiring leaders and seasoned executives, awaited a discourse on strategies and success. However, Sarah chose to steer the conversation towards a more introspective examination of wisdom and knowledge.

She recounted an episode from her early days – a venture that promised to revolutionize the industry. Sarah and her team, buoyed by a string of successes, had embarked on this project with unshakeable confidence in their collective expertise. But as the project unfolded, it became apparent that their confidence had blinded them to the complexities and unforeseen challenges they faced. The project teetered on the brink of failure, saved only by a last-minute pivot that was as much to do with luck as it was skill.

This experience served to create the foundation of Sarah's leadership philosophy. She introduced her audience to the Socratic paradox: the insight that 'I know that I know nothing'. It was a principle that seemed antithetical to the ethos of an industry driven by knowledge and certainty. Yet, for Sarah, it encapsulated the true essence of wisdom. The realization that her knowledge had limits and that acknowledging these limits could be a source of strength had been a turning point in her career.

Sarah argued that the tech industry, with its rapid pace and inherent unpredictability, demanded a leadership approach grounded in humility and the willingness to question. The Socratic paradox, with its emphasis on awareness of one's own ignorance, encouraged a culture of continuous learning and openness to new ideas. In recognizing what one did not know, one could find a deeper and more resilient form of wisdom.

As the seminar concluded, she realized her message had resonated with her audience, challenging their perceptions of knowledge and leadership. She had not only shared the lessons of her own journey but had also illuminated a more reflective and adaptive approach to navigating the uncertainties of the tech world.

In embracing the wisdom of uncertainty, Sarah had reaffirmed her place as a luminary in the industry. But more importantly, she had fostered a dialogue on the nature of wisdom itself; one that underscored the value of questioning and the virtue of recognizing our fallibility. This dialogue, rooted in the Socratic paradox, promised to inspire a new generation of leaders, equipped not just with the tools of technology but with the philosophical insights to wield them wisely.

The Socratic Paradox

The Socratic paradox was famously encapsulated in Socrates' assertion: 'I know that I know nothing'. This profound insight into the nature of knowledge and wisdom is not a declaration of total ignorance but an acknowledgment of the vastness of the unknown. It lies at the heart of intellectual humility, suggesting that true wisdom comes from recognizing the limits of our understanding and maintaining a curious and questioning mindset.

Socrates, through dialogues recorded by his student Plato, demonstrated that claiming absolute knowledge on complex subjects like justice, virtue or beauty often leads to contradictions. His method of elenchus, or Socratic questioning, was designed to reveal the inadequacies of supposed knowledge, pushing individuals towards deeper inquiry and reflection.

In contemporary contexts, the Socratic paradox serves as a reminder of the dangers of overconfidence. In complex and rapidly changing fields such as science, medicine and technology, where knowledge is constantly evolving, embracing the limits of our understanding can drive innovation and prevent the stagnation of ideas. It encourages professionals to remain open to new information, cultivate resilience in the face of uncertainty, challenge their own preconceptions and engage in lifelong learning and development. This fosters a culture of adaptability and continuous improvement.

Questions for Self-Reflection

1. **Embracing Uncertainty:** Reflect on a time when acknowledging what you didn't know led to a significant learning opportunity or a better decision. How did this experience change your approach to leadership or problem-solving?

2. **Facing Complex Challenges:** Consider the last time you faced a complex challenge at work. Did you feel pressured to have all the answers? How might embracing the Socratic paradox have impacted the outcome?

3. **Learning from Overconfidence:** Think about a situation where overconfidence in your knowledge or your team's expertise led to an oversight. What lessons did you learn about the value of questioning and critical thinking?

4. **Cultivating Intellectual Humility:** Evaluate your current practices. Do they foster continuous learning and intellectual humility within your team? How can you encourage a culture where acknowledging the limits of one's knowledge is seen as a strength rather than a weakness?

5. **Admitting Ignorance to Innovate:** Reflect on the role of the Socratic paradox in innovation and creativity. How can admitting 'I don't know' be a powerful starting point for exploring new ideas and solutions?

XXIII. ZERO-RISK BIAS

The Safe Bet

In the world of high finance, Thomas Baxter was a name that commanded respect. He was a portfolio manager with years of experience and a track record that spoke to his skill and caution. Thomas had navigated the turbulent waters of the stock market with a steady hand, always keeping his clients' investments safe from the stormy seas of market volatility. His philosophy had always been one of balance and prudence, and this had served him and his clients well over the years. However, as dark clouds began to gather on the economic horizon, Thomas found himself facing a dilemma that challenged the very foundations of his approach.

The impending economic downturn was unlike anything Thomas had faced before. The usual strategies and analyses seemed inadequate in the face of such unprecedented uncertainty. It was in this climate of fear and potential financial ruin that Thomas contemplated a radical departure from his time-tested approach. The idea of shifting a significant portion of his clients' diversified portfolios into zero-risk government bonds presented itself as a way to completely eliminate the risk of loss. They would act as a safe harbour in a time when the market seemed poised on the edge of a precipice.

This decision was not made lightly. Thomas wrestled with the implications, fully aware that his reputation for cautious, balanced investing was at stake. Yet, the thought of guaranteeing the safety of his clients' capital was ultimately too compelling to ignore.

The reaction from his clients was mixed. Some saw this move as a masterstroke, a bold decision to protect their investments when others seemed paralyzed by fear. Others, however, expressed concern. They worried that in the quest for safety, Thomas was sacrificing the potential for growth; that his zero-risk approach would leave them unable to capitalize on the market's recovery.

As the months turned into years, the economic downturn began to recede, giving way to a gradual but steady recovery. The markets rebounded, and the portfolios that had remained diversified began to see substantial growth. Thomas watched as these investments outpaced his zero-risk strategy, which, safe as it was, offered only modest returns in comparison.

The realization dawned on Thomas that in his effort to eliminate risk entirely, he had also closed the door on opportunity. Although his strategy had removed uncertainty and offered security, it had become a constraint, a barrier that prevented his clients from enjoying the fruits of the market's recovery. His zero-risk bias, once a source of comfort, had morphed into a lesson on the limitations of seeking absolute certainty in the unpredictable world of finance.

Reflecting on this period, Thomas recognized the value of balance and the necessity of embracing some level of risk as an inherent part of growth. The pursuit of a risk-free investment, while appealing in unpredictable times, ignored the dynamic nature of the markets and its potential for recovery and growth. This experience taught Thomas a valuable lesson that he would always carry with him about the complexities of investment strategy and the nuanced balance between risk and reward.

Zero-Risk Bias

Zero-risk bias describes someone's preference to eliminate risk entirely rather than reduce it, even when risk reduction is statistically more advantageous. It illustrates how the prospect of achieving a zero-risk status can be disproportionately appealing, often leading to decisions that aren't optimal in the long run.

This bias is rooted in the human aversion to loss and uncertainty. From a psychological perspective, the idea of eliminating risk entirely offers a sense of security and control, which can be particularly enticing in situations of stress or unpredictability. This desire for absolute safety can overshadow rational decision-making processes, leading individuals to overlook or undervalue opportunities for greater reward that come with manageable risks.

In finance, as seen with Thomas, zero-risk bias can lead to overly conservative investment strategies that sacrifice potential gains for the sake of avoiding losses. In public policy, this bias can result in the allocation of disproportionate resources to eliminate small risks, ignoring larger, more impactful risks that could be reduced more efficiently. In personal decision-making, it might manifest in choices that prioritize complete safety over potentially beneficial opportunities that carry some level of risk.

Here are some tools to help you mitigate zero-risk bias:

- **Risk Assessment:** Evaluating both the probabilities and impacts of various risks can provide a more balanced perspective than simply aiming to eliminate risk altogether.

- **Long-Term Planning:** Focusing on long-term goals and outcomes can help individuals and organizations weigh the trade-offs between risk elimination and potential rewards.

- **Diversification:** In finance and other decision-making arenas, diversification can reduce exposure to any single risk without having to resort to zero-risk options that may limit growth.

Questions for Self-Reflection

1. **The Impact of Zero-Risk Decisions:** Have you ever chosen a zero-risk option in your personal or professional life, sacrificing potential benefits for the sake of safety? Reflect on the outcome of that decision.

2. **Opting for Risk Reduction:** Consider a situation where *reducing* risk, rather than eliminating it, could have led to a better overall outcome. What prevented you from choosing the risk-reduction option?

3. **Responding to Stressful Scenarios:** Think about your response to uncertain or stressful situations. Do you find yourself gravitating towards zero-risk solutions? How does this affect your decision-making process?

4. **Balancing Risk and Reward:** Reflect on a decision where you successfully balanced risk and reward. What factors influenced

your decision-making process, and how can you apply these lessons to future decisions?

5. **Improving Risk Management Strategies:** Evaluate your current strategies for managing risk. How can you incorporate a more nuanced understanding of zero-risk bias to make more balanced and forward-thinking decisions?

XXIX. THE PLANNING FALLACY

The Deadline Dilemma

In the dynamic world of digital marketing, Laura Wilson was a name synonymous with creativity and resilience. As a seasoned project manager at a leading firm, she had steered her team through countless campaigns, each a testament to their ingenuity and unwavering commitment to excellence. With a track record of success, Laura approached every project with a confidence born of experience, certain in her team's ability to deliver outstanding results, even under the most pressing deadlines.

The latest challenge was a high-profile product launch – a project that promised to not only test their skills but also showcase their capacity for innovation. The client, impressed by Laura's portfolio, set an ambitious four-week timeline, confident in her team's ability to bring the vision to life. Buoyed by past triumphs, Laura embraced the challenge, her optimism undimmed by the daunting schedule. She believed fervently that her team would rise to the occasion, transforming obstacles into stepping stones towards success.

As the project unfolded, the first signs of trouble appeared. A vital member of the team was taken out of operation by illness, and a key software tool required an unforeseen update, threatening to disrupt the workflow. Laura, ever the stalwart leader, reassured her team and the client that these were mere bumps in the road. Drawing on their history of overcoming challenges, she maintained that the timeline was still achievable, her confidence serving as a beacon of hope for her team.

However, as the weeks slipped by, the obstacles grew, not just in number but in complexity. Vendor delays tangled their schedules, feedback loops spiraled into time-consuming revisions and last-minute client requests complicated their task. Despite the team's Herculean effort, working tirelessly through nights and weekends, the project veered off its charted course. The deadline loomed large; an insurmountable peak that remained out of reach.

The missed launch date was a sobering moment for Laura. In the aftermath, as she reflected on the project, it became clear that her initial optimism, while a source of strength, had also been a blind spot. Her confidence in the team's ability to navigate challenges had led her to underestimate the impact of unforeseen issues. The optimistic timeline, which had seemed attainable in the glow of past successes, had not accounted for the inevitable snags that accompany complex digital marketing projects.

This realization marked a turning point for Laura. It underscored the importance of balancing optimism with realism, of tempering confidence with careful planning and contingencies for the unexpected and of being ready to pivot when the path forward becomes obstructed. Laura recognized that true leadership in the fast-paced world of digital marketing required not just faith in her team's abilities but also a willingness to confront potential problems head-on, plan for them and adapt strategies accordingly.

For Laura and her team, the project was a lesson in humility and growth. It became a catalyst for refining their approach and integrating more robust planning and risk management strategies to navigate the complexities of their industry. In the end, it provided the path to greater wisdom and resilience, a reminder that the journey to success is as much about preparation and adaptability as it is about confidence and creativity.

The Planning Fallacy

The planning fallacy, a term coined by psychologists Daniel Kahneman and Amos Tversky in 1979, describes a cognitive bias that leads people to underestimate the time, costs and risks of future actions while overestimating the benefits. This bias affects both personal and professional realms, from simple daily tasks to complex projects like Laura's marketing campaign.

At its core, the planning fallacy is rooted in optimism bias and an overconfidence in our own abilities, with individuals naturally inclined to view their future endeavours through a rose-coloured lens. This optimistic outlook often disregards statistical realities observed in similar past projects, leading to overly ambitious timelines and budgets.

Several factors contribute to the planning fallacy:

- **Insufficient Consideration of Past Experiences:** Individuals often fail to accurately incorporate lessons from previous similar activities, focusing instead on best-case scenarios.

- **Focus on the Ideal Path:** Planners tend to envision the smoothest route to project completion, ignoring potential disruptions and the non-linear nature of most tasks.

- **Misunderstanding of Probabilistic Outcomes:** There's a common neglect of the probabilistic nature of tasks and deadlines, where unforeseen complications are not just possible but likely.

- **Motivational Factors:** Sometimes, the desire to please stakeholders or win competitive bids can lead to deliberately aggressive timelines. In these cases, we hope for the best outcome rather than making objective predictions.

Strategies to mitigate the planning fallacy involve both psychological adjustments and practical project management techniques:

- **Reference Class Forecasting:** By systematically reviewing similar past projects (reference classes) and their actual timelines and budgets, planners can base estimates on statistical realities rather than optimism.

- **Implementing a Buffer:** Adding a buffer to your schedule to account for unforeseen delays can provide a more realistic timeline.

- **Breaking Down Tasks:** Detailed breakdowns of tasks can reveal complexities that might be overlooked in broad estimates.

- **Seeking External Perspectives:** External evaluations can provide objective insights that counteract the team's inherent optimism.

Questions for Self-Reflection

1. **Learning from the Planning Fallacy:** Reflect on a project where you fell victim to the planning fallacy. What were the optimistic assumptions you made, and how did reality differ?

2. **Historical Data vs Ideal Scenarios:** Consider the role of past experiences in your planning process. Are there instances where you ignored historical data in favour of an ideal scenario?

3. **Buffers and External Insights:** How can implementing a buffer in your schedule or seeking external perspectives change the outcome of your future projects?

4. **Psychological Influences:** Reflect on the psychological factors, such as the desire to please or compete, that may influence your project planning. How can you mitigate these influences?

5. **Task Complexity and Detailed Analysis:** Think about the breakdown of tasks in your last project. Did a detailed analysis reveal complexities you hadn't initially considered? How will this insight affect your future planning approach?

XXX. THE ENDOWMENT EFFECT

The Untraded Heirloom

Margaret had inherited a quaint, rustic cottage from her grandparents, nestled in the serene countryside of New England. It was a modest dwelling, surrounded by sprawling fields and a small, tranquil pond that reflected the changing skies. For Margaret, the cottage was more than just property; it was a repository of cherished childhood memories, a symbol of her family's legacy and a tangible connection to her late grandparents.

Over the years, Margaret had meticulously maintained the cottage, preserving its original charm while making necessary updates. She spent countless weekends there, often alone, sometimes with close friends or family, relishing the quietude and simplicity it offered away from her bustling city life.

One autumn, a renowned real estate developer discovered the area and proposed to build a luxury resort nearby. As news of the development spread, property values in the region began to soar. Margaret received an unsolicited offer for the cottage at a price that far exceeded its market value before the resort's announcement. It presented a significant financial opportunity, one that could secure her financial future and fulfil her long-standing dreams, like traveling the world and supporting charitable causes dear to her heart.

Yet, the thought of selling the cottage filled Margaret with a profound sense of loss. It wasn't just summer days spent under the old oak tree or the crisp, starry nights by the pond that she would miss; it was the loss of a piece of her identity, a tangible link to her past and the generations that came before her. The decision weighed heavily on her. She was torn between the logic of accepting the offer and the emotional pull to hold onto the cottage.

The Endowment Effect

The emotional turmoil Margaret experienced is a classic manifestation of the endowment effect, a phenomenon that significantly impacts our decision-making process regarding possessions. This cognitive bias leads us to value items we own more highly than those we do not, simply because we own them. But why does this happen, and what implications does it have for our behaviour?

The endowment effect was first extensively studied and brought to public attention by economists like Richard Thaler, who noted the discrepancy between the valuation of items by sellers and buyers. Several theories have been proposed to explain its psychological underpinnings. One prominent idea revolves around the idea of loss aversion, as introduced by Daniel Kahneman and Amos Tversky. This theory posits that individuals inherently prefer avoiding losses to acquiring equivalent gains. When applied to the endowment effect, this means that the potential loss felt by parting with an owned item (such as Margaret's cottage) is perceived as more significant than the benefit gained from selling it, even if the sale is financially advantageous.

Another explanation focuses on the sense of ownership and identity. Objects we own become extensions of ourselves, intertwined with our identity and personal history. This emotional attachment imbues the object with value beyond its physical attributes or market price, as seen in Margaret's deep connection to her cottage.

Research in behavioural economics and psychology has provided empirical evidence supporting the endowment effect. Experiments often demonstrate that individuals assign higher value to objects as soon as they take ownership, a pattern consistent across various contexts, from simple mugs and pens in laboratory settings to real estate and stocks in financial markets.

The endowment effect influences a wide range of behaviours and decisions, from personal property sales, like Margaret's dilemma, to investment trading and consumer purchases. Understanding this bias helps explain why people often hold onto stocks or real estate longer than is economically rational or why consumers prefer products they already own over potentially better alternatives.

Critics of the endowment effect as a concept argue that some observed behaviours attributed to it might instead result from other factors, such as transaction costs, strategic behaviour in bargaining or the misinterpretation of preferences. However, the bulk of the evidence supports its significant role in behavioural economics and its relevance in understanding and predicting economic behaviour.

Questions for Self-Reflection

1. **Rejecting Generous Offers:** Have you ever turned down an offer to sell something you owned, even though the offer was objectively generous? What motivated your decision?

2. **Sentimental Value and Worth Perception:** Think about an item you own that holds sentimental value. How do you think this emotional attachment influences your perception of its worth?

3. **The Influence of Ownership:** Consider a time when you had to decide whether to keep or sell an investment (e.g., stocks, real estate). How did your sense of ownership affect your decision-making process?

4. **Post-Purchase Valuation:** Reflect on your purchasing decisions. Do you find yourself valuing items more after you've purchased them? How does this affect your buying behaviour?

5. **Making Decisions with Emotional Stakes:** Imagine you are in Margaret's situation. How would you approach the decision to sell or keep the cottage? What factors would weigh most heavily on your decision-making process?

XXXI. PAREIDOLIA

Visions in the Void

Vincent Marlowe, a name revered in the halls of astrophysics, had reached the pinnacle of his career through a relentless pursuit of one of humanity's most elusive questions: are we alone in the universe? His life's work, the search for extraterrestrial intelligence, was a testament to his unwavering commitment to this quest. Day after day, Vincent sat before his instruments, his eyes tracing the faint glow of screens, his ears tuned to the subtle whispers of the cosmos, sifting through the cacophony of cosmic noise for a sign, any sign, that might betray the presence of another living thing.

It was on a night like any other, under a serene blanket of stars, that Vincent's routine vigil was shattered by a revelation. As he analysed the data from a recent deep space observation, what he found amidst the usual static was anything but mundane. There, on his screen, emerged a pattern so distinct, so startlingly clear, that it seemed to pierce the veil of solitude that enveloped humanity's existence in the universe. A face, if it could be called that, gazed back at him from the depths of space, its features eerily symmetrical, hauntingly familiar in their approximation to human form. A shiver cascaded through Vincent's body, a primal reaction to coming face-to-face with the unknown.

Driven by a mixture of scientific duty and an unshakable sense of wonder, Vincent took his discovery to the broader scientific community. He presented his findings with the careful precision of a seasoned astrophysicist. Yet, beneath his composed exterior lay a tumult of excitement and apprehension. The response was as immediate as it was divided. Debates ignited within academic circles, splitting the community into factions. Some dismissed the image as a fluke, a trick of light and shadow, and no more significant than seeing shapes in clouds. Others, however, sensed the gravity of Vincent's discovery, considering it perhaps the first tangible evidence of intelligent life beyond Earth.

Vincent found himself standing on the precipice of the unknown, his discovery challenging the very foundations of scientific understanding. The face from the void became a mirror reflecting the dual nature of humanity's quest for knowledge: the rigorous scepticism that is the hallmark of science pitted against the deep-seated yearning to find connection – to know that in the vast, indifferent universe, humanity is not alone. Vincent's discovery served as a poignant reminder of the eternal tension between doubt and belief, between the familiar and the unimaginable.

As the debate raged on, Vincent continued his work, undeterred. The face he had seen, whether a quirk of data or a beacon from distant neighbours, had rekindled the flame of curiosity that had driven him into the arms of the cosmos in the first place. It stood as a beacon, reminding him and the world that the quest for knowledge is, at its heart, a journey defined by the courage to confront the unknown and to ask questions that might forever change our place in the universe.

Pareidolia

Pareidolia represents a psychological phenomenon where the mind perceives recognizable shapes and patterns, particularly faces, within unrelated stimuli. It is a type of apophenia, which is the broader term for seeing patterns in random data. The phenomenon is not merely about visual fallacies; it touches on the deeply ingrained human tendency to seek meaning in our environment, a trait that has been both a survival mechanism and a source of myth-making throughout history.

The science behind pareidolia reveals much about our perceptual processes. Humans are wired for pattern recognition, a skill that has historically conferred advantages, such as the ability to recognize faces quickly, identify predators in the wild or read emotions. The fusiform gyrus, part of the brain's visual system, is specifically tuned to detect faces, explaining why facial pareidolia is so common.

Neurologically, when visual information is incomplete or ambiguous, the brain's pattern-recognition system fills in the gaps, drawing from memory and expectation. This is why people can often perceive familiar figures in random noise, texture on rocks or clouds in the sky.

Pareidolia has intriguing implications across various domains. In the arts, it spurs creativity, inspiring artists to incorporate or elaborate on the shapes they perceive in random textures or landscapes. In everyday life, it can manifest in harmless ways, such as seeing the 'man in the moon', but it can also contribute to superstitious beliefs or conspiracy theories when individuals attribute undue significance to the patterns they perceive.

Understanding pareidolia is also crucial in the age of machine learning and computer vision. As AI systems are trained to process visual data, distinguishing between genuine patterns and pareidolia is a significant challenge. For scientists like Vincent, recognizing pareidolia is essential to avoid false positives in data analysis, ensuring that interpretations remain grounded in verifiable patterns.

Questions for Self-Reflection

1. **Pattern Recognition in Market Data:** Reflect on a time when you thought you saw a clear pattern or trend in the market data. Was it a genuine indicator of market direction, or could it have been financial pareidolia? How did you validate your observation before acting on it?

2. **Investment Decisions and Confirmation Bias:** Consider how pareidolia might interplay with confirmation bias in your investment analysis. Have you ever favoured information that aligned with your market predictions while potentially overlooking data that didn't?

3. **Risk of Overfitting in Algorithmic Trading:** If you utilize algorithmic trading or data models, think about the potential for overfitting to perceived patterns in historical data. How do you ensure that your models are identifying real trends and not just financial 'noise'?

4. **Assessing Unconventional Investments:** When evaluating unconventional or speculative investments, how can you differentiate between genuine opportunity and seeing 'faces in the clouds'? What checks and balances do you have in place to avoid being misled by illusory patterns?

5. **Diversification Strategy:** How might pareidolia affect your approach to diversification? Are there instances where you

might perceive correlations between assets that are not actually related, and how does this perception influence your portfolio construction?

XXXII. THE CAUSALITY FALLACY

The Market's Invisible Hand

In the heart of a sprawling metropolis, amidst the towering skyscrapers of the financial district, there lived a trader named Robert. With a career spanning several decades, Robert had become something of a legend on the trading floor. His peers often marvelled at his ability to read the market's subtle signs, to sense its rhythm like a seasoned conductor leading an orchestra. His experience had not only sharpened his skills but had also imbued him with an intuitive understanding of the market's unpredictable nature.

During a particularly tumultuous week, when the market took a sharp and unforeseen dive, the trading floor was abuzz with speculation and confusion. Analysts and traders alike scrambled to make sense of the situation, poring over economic reports and world news, trying to pinpoint the cause of the sudden downturn. Suggestions ranged from rising geopolitical tensions in key regions to surprising shifts in economic indicators and downturns in specific industry sectors. Yet, amidst this cacophony of theories and conjectures, there was no clear consensus, no singular event that they could definitively blame for the upheaval.

Amid this uncertainty, Robert stepped forward with a theory of his own. He pointed to a recent international trade deal that had unexpectedly fallen through – a deal that many had not considered to be of significance until now. Robert, drawing on his vast experience, recalled similar instances in the past where failed deals had led to market volatility. He articulated his thoughts with such confidence and clarity, drawing direct lines between this event and the current market conditions, that his theory quickly gained traction. Before long, his perspective was being echoed by traders throughout the floor, and it even found its way into the narratives spun by financial news networks. This explanation, singular and straightforward, began to shape the investment strategies of countless traders, all looking for a way to navigate the market's stormy waters.

However, as the weeks passed and more detailed analyses emerged, a different picture began to take shape. It became apparent that the downturn was the result of a complex interplay of factors, each relatively minor on its own but significant in their collective impact. The much-discussed trade deal, while certainly a factor, was far from being the primary cause it was characterised as. Instead, it was just one piece in a much larger puzzle, a puzzle that included subtle shifts in market sentiment, minor disruptions in supply chains and even changes in consumer behaviour across different regions.

This revelation prompted a moment of introspection for Robert and many of his peers. It served as a stark reminder of the market's inherent complexity, a system influenced by an array of factors, both large and small. Robert's inclination to find a singular cause – a need for clarity in a world often governed by chance and complexity – had led him to craft a narrative that was compelling, yet overly simplistic.

The experience was humbling, not just for Robert but for the entire trading floor. It underscored the dangers of oversimplification and the human tendency to seek straightforward explanations for phenomena that are inherently complex. For Robert, it was a reminder that even the most seasoned traders are not immune to the market's capacity to surprise and confound. It reinforced the value of maintaining a broad perspective, of considering a multitude of factors before drawing conclusions and of the importance of continuous learning in this ever-evolving landscape.

The Causality Fallacy

The causality fallacy is a cognitive bias that compels individuals to find simple explanations for complex events. It's the tendency to assume a direct cause-and-effect relationship even when the connection is not substantiated by evidence. This bias reflects our discomfort with uncertainty and our desire for the world to be orderly and predictable.

Humans are naturally inclined to seek patterns and causal relationships. This tendency has evolutionary roots as understanding cause and effect has been critical for our survival. In modern times, however, this can lead to incorrect assumptions and judgments. The need for causality is particularly pronounced in environments like financial markets, where uncertainty is high and the stakes are significant.

This bias is reinforced by several factors:

- **Pattern Recognition:** Our brains are wired to recognize patterns, which can lead to perceiving connections where none exist.

- **Simplification:** Simple narratives are easier to grasp and more comfortable to deal with than complex, multifaceted realities.

- **The Illusion of Control:** Believing we understand the causes of events gives us a sense of control, even if that understanding is flawed.

For investors, the need to understand causality can lead to oversimplified investment theses, underestimation of market complexity and overconfidence in their predictive abilities. It can result in mispricing of assets, herd behaviour and potentially significant financial missteps. Investors can counteract this bias by using these approaches:

- **Diversifying Sources:** Consulting multiple sources of information will provide a more nuanced view of market events.

- **Embracing Complexity:** We must accept the reality that market movements can result from many interrelated factors rather than a single cause.

- **Seeking Contradictory Evidence:** Actively looking for information that challenges our belief in cause-and-effect relationships will help us tackle our bias.

Questions for Self-Reflection

1. **Reevaluating Causes:** Recall a time when you attributed a market event to a single cause. In hindsight, was this attribution accurate, or were there other contributing factors?

2. **Complexity in Investment Analysis:** How do you ensure that your investment analysis accounts for the complexity of

market dynamics rather than relying on simplistic explanations?

3. **Challenging Cause-and-Effect Assumptions:** Consider an investment decision you made based on a perceived cause-and-effect relationship. Did you seek out contradictory evidence, and how might that have changed your decision?

4. **Causality and Confidence:** Reflect on how the need to understand causality has influenced your confidence in predicting market movements. Has this led to overconfidence in certain strategies?

5. **Mitigating the Causality Fallacy:** What steps can you take to prevent the causality fallacy from impacting your financial decision-making in the future?

XXIII. TELEOLOGICAL THINKING

Blinded by a Vision of the Future

Maxwell, a distinguished figure in the venture capital world, was renowned for his financial acumen as well as his uncanny ability to spot the next big thing in the startup ecosystem. His investment philosophy was rooted in a simple yet profound belief: the key to a startup's success lay in its vision for the future. To Maxwell, a startup was more than its current valuation or product lineup; it was a vehicle for realizing a bold, transformative vision. He firmly believed that companies with a compelling end goal had the potential to redefine industries as well as succeed on their own terms.

This belief guided Maxwell's approach to investment, leading him to back ventures that promised not just financial returns but also a chance to shape the future. His portfolio was a testament to this strategy, filled with companies at the forefront of innovation in their respective fields.

Then came the pitch that seemed to embody everything Maxwell looked for in an investment. A tech startup, with aspirations to redefine human interaction within the home, presented a concept that was both inventive and transformative. The founders spoke with passion, not about the immediate road to profitability or strategies for capturing market share but about a future where technology was woven into the very fabric of everyday life. They envisioned a world in which technology made life more convenient but also enriched human relationships and wellbeing. Maxwell was captivated. Here was a company that aligned perfectly with his investment philosophy – a startup not just aiming for success in the market but striving to usher in a new era of human-centric technology.

Eager to be part of this ambitious venture, Maxwell decided to invest heavily, convinced that the startup's transformative potential was worth the risk. His belief in the power of a compelling vision to drive success was unwavering.

However, as months turned into years, the anticipated breakthroughs failed to materialize, and the startup struggled to gain traction. Despite its visionary goals, the company faced significant challenges in execution. User interface design was clunky and failed to resonate with users, while customer acquisition strategies were inadequate, failing to convey the life-changing potential of the technology to a broader audience. The startup's focus on the end goal, while noble, had led it to overlook the practical steps needed to finesse day-to-day operations and ensure growth.

This disconnect between vision and execution became a critical stumbling block. The founders' single-minded focus on their long-term vision had blinded them to the importance of addressing the immediate, practical concerns essential for building a successful company. User experience, market fit and effective go-to-market strategies – elements crucial to the survival of any tech venture – had been neglected in favour of pursuing an image of the future that seemed increasingly distant.

For Maxwell, this experience was a profound lesson in the complexities of startup success. It highlighted the delicate balance between vision and execution, between dreaming of the future and navigating the realities of the present. The startup's struggles underscored the necessity of coupling novel ideas with a pragmatic approach to business development.

Reflecting on this investment, Maxwell recognized the need to adapt his philosophy. While a compelling vision remained a critical indicator of a startup's potential, it was clear that vision alone was not enough. Success in the volatile world of startups required a harmonious blend of future-oriented thinking and meticulous attention to the operational and strategic details that enable a company to move forward.

This realization did not diminish Maxwell's enthusiasm for visionary startups but rather enriched his approach to venture capital. He became more attuned to the balance between the end goal and the means of achieving it, looking for teams that not only dreamed big but also had a clear plan for making their vision a reality. His experience with the tech startup, while not the success he had hoped for, provided Maxwell with invaluable insights that would inform his investment decisions for years to come.

Teleological Thinking

Teleological thinking, often involved in proportionality bias, is the tendency to ascribe a purpose, goal or end (telos) to actions, objects or phenomena. This type of thinking is natural for humans – we often look for the intentions or purpose behind things to make sense of the world around us.

Teleological thinking can be traced back to our cognitive development as children, where we learn to understand the world by attributing purposes to the things we see and experience. It's reinforced by our inherent search for meaning and our comfort with narratives that suggest a clear direction or reason for existence.

In the context of investments and business, teleological thinking can lead to a bias where the end goals of a company are given undue weight in decision-making, sometimes at the expense of practical and immediate considerations that are crucial for the company's survival and growth.

For investors like Maxwell, teleological thinking resulted in him becoming too focused on the ultimate goals of the company and ignoring the operational steps required to achieve those goals. This bias can affect due diligence, leading to investments that seem promising on a visionary level but are less viable in terms of practical execution.

Investors can counteract this bias by using these tools:

- **Balancing Vision with Execution:** While a company's vision is important, equal weight should be given to its ability to execute day-to-day operations.

- **Incremental Milestones:** Evaluating a company's track record in achieving incremental milestones can provide a more grounded perspective on its potential to achieve its goals.

- **Cross-Disciplinary Teams:** Encouraging cross-disciplinary perspectives in investment teams can ensure that both visionary and practical aspects are considered.

Questions for Self-Reflection

1. **Balancing Vision and Execution:** When evaluating a potential investment, how do you balance the weight you give to the company's ultimate goals with the practical means by which it plans to achieve them?

2. **End Goal vs Operational Capabilities:** Can you recall an investment that was driven more by the end goal of the business than its operational capabilities? What was the outcome, and what did you learn?

3. **Ignoring Short-Term Challenges:** How can you ensure that teleological thinking does not lead you to underestimate the importance of short-term challenges and operational hurdles in a startup's journey?

4. **Due Diligence:** Reflect on the role of due diligence in mitigating the risks associated with teleological thinking. What specific practices could help you assess whether a company's vision is matched by its capacity for execution?

5. **Reassessing Teleological Decisions:** Consider a past investment that did not meet expectations. In retrospect, was teleological thinking at play, and how might a different approach have altered your decision-making?

XXXIV. THE HOT HAND FALLACY

The Streak of Success

In the bustling heart of the financial district, where the air buzzes with the electric hum of trading and the rapid exchange of fortunes, Damian had carved out a reputation that was nothing short of legendary. Known among his peers on the trading floor for his knack for picking stocks that delivered growth, Damian's success story had become a beacon for many. Over recent months, his selections had consistently outperformed market expectations, earning him the awe and admiration of colleagues and clients alike. They whispered his name with a mix of respect and envy, attributing his uncanny success to a blend of skill, intuition and an almost prophetic insight into market trends.

This period of remarkable success, often referred to as Damian's 'hot streak', had not only bolstered his confidence but had also drawn in a following. Novice traders, attracted by the allure of his Midas touch, began to mirror his trades in the hope of replicating his success. The logic was seductively simple: if Damian was investing in a stock, its success was almost guaranteed.

Yet, the financial markets, with their inherent unpredictability, were about to deliver a stark lesson. Damian's latest selection, a tech startup touted as the next big disruptor within its industry, suddenly plummeted following the revelation of a major scandal. This unforeseen downturn sent shockwaves through the trading floor, leaving Damian and his legion of followers grappling with substantial losses.

The fallout from this ill-fated pick was immediate and profound. For those who had placed their trust – and their capital – in Damian's seemingly infallible judgment, the disappointment was a bitter pill to swallow. This turn of events forced a moment of reckoning, not just for Damian but for all who had followed him, highlighting the perils of relying too heavily on the alluring idea of a 'winning streak'.

Damian, once celebrated for his unerring market instincts, found himself at a crossroads. The incident served as a sobering reminder of the fickle nature of success, the market's volatility and the dangers of speculative trading based on personal success narratives rather than on thorough, fundamental analysis. It was a humbling experience that challenged the very foundation of his trading philosophy, prompting him to reassess his approach. However, by reminding him that true success comes not from riding waves of popularity or temporary market trends but from a deep, nuanced understanding of the markets and a disciplined approach to investment, it was a catalyst for growth. Moving forward, he committed to balancing his intuitive picks with a more rigorous approach, aiming to not only reclaim his reputation but also to serve as a more grounded example for others.

For Damian's followers, it was equally eye-opening. It underscored the risks associated with blindly following the trades of others, no matter how successful they appeared to be. The allure of quick gains, they realized, often came with overlooked risks, especially when investments were made without a personal understanding of the complex market forces at play and the inherent uncertainty in trading.

Damian's meteoric rise and sobering fall marked a pivotal moment of reflection within the trading community, sparking discussions about the nature of success in trading and the importance of education and due diligence. For novice traders, it was a lesson in personal accountability and the value of building a solid foundation of market knowledge and analytical skills, rather than riding on the coattails of others.

The Hot Hand Fallacy

The hot hand fallacy reflects our intuitive yet often misguided belief in 'streaks' within independent random events. This bias is not confined to sports or gambling but extends into various domains, including financial markets, where it can significantly influence investor behaviour and decision-making strategies.

The term 'hot hand' originated in the realm of sports, particularly in basketball, to describe the phenomenon where players are perceived to have a higher probability of scoring if they have made previous successful shots. This belief suggests that success breeds further success in a short sequence of attempts, leading observers and even players to expect continued performance above the norm.

Psychologically, the hot hand fallacy arises from a human tendency to see patterns and sequences in data where none exist. This is a manifestation of the clustering illusion, a cognitive bias where individuals overinterpret random data to perceive patterns. The human brain is wired to seek order and predictability in the environment, an evolutionary trait that, historically, has served to help us recognize food sources, predators and other elements essential to our survival. In modern contexts, however, this predisposition can lead to erroneous conclusions about causality and probability.

Initial studies in the 1980s, notably by Gilovich, Vallone and Tversky, found no statistical evidence supporting the hot hand in basketball, suggesting that each shot is independent of the last. However, subsequent research and advanced analyses have provided more nuance, indicating that, in certain contexts, players might indeed exhibit streaks that are not entirely explained by randomness.

In financial markets, the hot hand fallacy can be seen when investors expect that stocks, funds or traders will continue to perform well based on recent successes. This belief often overlooks the principle that past performance is not indicative of future results, a cornerstone of financial theory which posits that market movements are largely unpredictable and influenced by a myriad of factors.

The fallacy can lead investors to make several key errors:

- **Chasing Performance:** Investors may select stocks or funds based on recent gains, expecting the trend to continue, which can lead to buying high and selling low.

- **Overconcentration:** Belief in the hot hand might cause investors to overconcentrate their portfolio on recent winners, increasing risk through lack of diversification.

- **Neglect of Fundamental Analysis:** The allure of continuing success may lead investors to disregard fundamental analysis, focusing instead on historical returns as a predictor of future performance.

Mitigating the hot hand fallacy in investment practices requires a disciplined, evidence-based approach:

- **Rational Perspective and Empirical Evidence:** Recognizing the inherent randomness in market returns and relying on empirical evidence can help investors maintain a rational perspective on performance streaks.

- **Long-term Perspective and Diversification:** Maintaining a long-term investment perspective and ensuring portfolio diversification can guard against the risks associated with chasing recent successes.

- **Behavioural Checks:** Implementing behavioural checks, such as waiting periods before making investment decisions based on recent trends, can help prevent impulsive decisions influenced by the hot hand belief.

Understanding the hot hand fallacy and its implications in financial decision-making underscores the importance of critical thinking and statistical literacy in navigating markets. By acknowledging the role of randomness and maintaining a disciplined approach to investment, individuals can mitigate the influence of this pervasive cognitive bias.

Questions for Self-Reflection

1. **Learning from Decisions Based on Streaks:** Have you ever made investment decisions based on a trader's or investment's recent success? What was the outcome, and what did you learn from it?

2. **Skill vs Luck:** How do you differentiate between genuine skill in stock selection and a lucky streak when evaluating your own investment decisions or those of others?

3. **Overcoming the Hot Hand Fallacy:** Reflect on a time when you succumbed to the hot hand fallacy. How can you ensure your investment strategy is more data-driven and less influenced by recent outcomes?

4. **Raising Awareness of the Hot Hand Fallacy:** What steps can you take to educate less experienced investors about the risks of following perceived hot hands in the market?

5. **The Impact on Risk Management:** How has understanding the hot hand fallacy changed your approach to risk assessment and portfolio management?

PART 2

EMOTIONAL BIASES

XXXV. LOSS AVERSION

A Slippery Slope

Mark, an experienced investment analyst with a stellar track record, faced an unusual dilemma. Several years ago, motivated by a belief in the long-term promise of emerging biofuel technologies, he had directed a significant portion of his personal portfolio towards shares in a promising but unproven startup called BioInnovate.

Initially, the investment brought him a wave of satisfaction. It wasn't just about potential financial returns but the feeling of contributing to an industry that might solve pressing environmental challenges. Yet, years passed, and BioInnovate faced repeated delays and setbacks. Competitors unveiled rival technologies, and research funding was tough to obtain. The stock Mark bought at a high price dwindled in value. On paper, he was now showing a significant loss.

Logically, Mark knew investment strategies evolve over time. His rigorous training taught him about sunk costs – resources already spent that should not factor into current or future decisions. Yet, a gnawing unease plagued him. Selling the stock would mean crystallizing that loss, admitting not just a financial miscalculation but also that his early belief in BioInnovate's vision was a mistake.

News headlines worsened the situation. A leading automotive company announced a partnership with one of BioInnovate's competitors, touting their planned mass-market electric vehicles. Analysts were abuzz with predictions about biofuels losing dominance far sooner than anticipated. Yet, something in Mark remained stubbornly defiant. He found himself digging through old industry reports, grasping at outdated data points to reassure himself the tide would inevitably turn in BioInnovate's favour.

One morning, while scanning the financial news, a different article caught Mark's eye. It profiled a fledgling solar cell company touting a disruptive design with potentially game-changing efficiency. This sparked a long-dormant excitement, reminiscent of when he first invested in BioInnovate. The article noted the solar company was seeking early-stage funding. Mark realized that to act on this new opportunity, he needed capital. The same capital that was currently tied up in his dwindling BioInnovate shares.

The decision felt agonizing. Should he cut his losses and move on? Or double down his commitment to BioInnovate in hopes of a future turnaround? Every night turned into a battleground in his mind between the two arguments. Deep down, he knew that his hesitation wasn't solely about past investment – it was something more visceral, a powerful resistance to the feeling of being wrong.

Loss Aversion

Mark's internal conflict highlights the pervasive power of loss aversion. This cognitive bias describes the strong human tendency to prioritize avoiding losses over acquiring equivalent gains. Psychological studies consistently demonstrate that the pain of a loss can feel roughly twice as intense as the joy of a comparable gain.

Understanding loss aversion requires untangling several elements:

- **Evolutionary Roots:** Our aversion to loss is embedded in ancient survival instincts. In earlier times, losing resources posed a direct threat to life and wellbeing. While most modern circumstances differ dramatically, our brains haven't entirely caught up, making us inherently more risk-averse when faced with a potential loss.
- **Framing Bias:** How a situation is presented strongly influences our perception of gains and losses. For example, accepting a definite small loss can feel worse than accepting the chance of a potentially larger loss, even if logically the outcome might be the same.
- **Reference Point Dependency:** Loss aversion hinges on our subjective reference points. A decline in value from when we initially bought a stock is psychologically harder to accept than if we acquired that same stock at the lower current price, even though, rationally, the situations are identical.
- **Emotional Weight:** Losses aren't merely a financial calculation; they activate emotional centres associated with fear, regret and even a sense of personal failure. This can cloud our objective decision-making abilities.

Loss aversion doesn't make us irrational; it highlights the difference between how we experience a situation emotionally and how we might analyse it intellectually. This internal conflict has far-reaching implications:

- **The Sunk Cost Fallacy:** Fear of accepting a definite loss leads to the sunk cost fallacy where we cling to failing ventures because we've already invested so much. But we can't recoup past investments in this way. Future decisions should be based on current merit, not the burden of previous miscalculations.

- **Status Quo Bias:** Loss aversion fuels a disproportionate preference for the current state of affairs. The potential pain of losing that familiarity, or the sense of control associated with a particular choice, can stop us making even beneficial changes.
- **Missed Opportunities:** While it's wise to be risk-aware, excessive loss aversion makes us blind to potentially greater gains found in unexplored territory. This applies to investments, careers and relationships.

Recognizing loss aversion's mechanisms is the first step towards mitigating its influence. We may not be able to eliminate these deeply ingrained human tendencies, but understanding them can empower us with informed awareness when facing complex choices.

Questions for Self-Reflection

1. **Sunk Costs in Your Life:** Can you identify situations where the sunk cost fallacy swayed your decisions? Were they investments of money, time or emotional energy?

2. **Disentangling Emotion:** When faced with a potential loss, how can you distinguish between rational analysis of risk and the pain of letting go?

3. **Reframing Failure:** Could viewing missteps as 'learning costs' rather than losses shift your aversion to taking risk?

4. **Focusing on Opportunity:** How can you retrain your mind to highlight the potential upside of change, even when it involves moving away from prior investments?

5. **The Cost of Indecision**: While avoiding a concrete loss can be tempting, have you considered the opportunity cost of sticking with the status quo?

XXXVI. THE DISPOSITION EFFECT

Holding On

Ben's tumultuous journey through the rocky terrain of the stock market had endowed him with the confidence to make bold decisions as well as wealth. Yet, despite this veneer of assurance, Ben found himself grappling with a perplexing pattern of behaviour that gradually began to erode his self-assuredness and, more critically, his portfolio's health.

This pattern manifested most clearly in his approach to managing successful investments. Logic and training dictated that he should sell these assets once they reached peak value, capitalizing on their success. However, Ben noticed a disconcerting reluctance to part with these winning stocks. Even as the market provided clear signals that it was time to harvest profits and redistribute assets, a deep-seated instinct urged him to cling to them, driven by a desire for even more gains. This was not mere greed but a visceral reaction to the prospect of letting go too soon.

The flipside of this dilemma was even more pronounced. When faced with declining stocks, Ben's reaction was not to cut losses but to double down on his commitment. This wasn't stubbornness but a profound aversion to admitting defeat. The thought of selling at a loss was so unpalatable that it clouded his judgment, convincing him, against all odds, that a turnaround was just around the corner. This tendency to hold onto losing investments for far too long, in the hope of recouping losses, was a stark deviation from rational investment strategy.

A particularly poignant episode underscored the detrimental impact of this behaviour. Ben had invested heavily in a tech startup, drawn by its innovative approach and explosive growth potential. As the startup's value skyrocketed, Ben's confidence swelled, and the euphoria of his apparent foresight blinded him to the strategic exit points that market indicators were suggesting. Focused on visions of grandeur, he watched passively as the market took a sudden, unexpected turn, and his profits began to evaporate. Yet, even as the reality of his dwindling investment set in, Ben found himself unable to sell, paralyzed by the hope that the market's favour would return.

In seeking to understand this self-sabotaging cycle, Ben stumbled upon the concept of the disposition effect. This cognitive bias encapsulated his irrational behaviour: an aversion to realizing losses coupled with an eagerness to continue riding the wave of gains until the market turns. The realization that his decisions were being undercut by this ingrained bias was a jolt to Ben. It highlighted a critical flaw in his investment approach – his emotional responses were undermining his logic.

Determined to break free from this cycle, Ben implemented a disciplined regimen for his future investments. He set concrete rule for himself on when to 'take profits' and 'stop loss' in each new venture; decisions made in the clarity of calm analysis rather than the fog of emotional turmoil. This systematized approach aimed to detach the decision-making process from the emotional weight of gains and losses, ensuring that his investment strategy remained aligned with his objectives and was not swayed by the disposition effect.

This shift marked a pivotal transformation in Ben's investment philosophy, underscoring the importance of discipline, foresight and, most crucially, the recognition of one's vulnerabilities. By confronting and mitigating the impact of the disposition effect, Ben not only safeguarded his portfolio against irrational decisions but also embarked on a path towards more resilient, informed investment practices.

The Disposition Effect

Ben's experiences underscore the insidious nature of the disposition effect, which plagues experienced and novice investors alike. The roots of this bias lie in a mix of powerful psychological phenomena:

- **Loss Aversion:** Humans feel the pain of losses more sharply than the satisfaction of gains. The prospect of turning a 'paper loss' into a tangible, realized loss creates a psychological barrier to selling, even when logic advises doing so.

- **The Sunk Cost Fallacy:** We become more reluctant to abandon a failing investment the more we've sunk into it, whether that's time, money or emotion. Rather than relying on rational analysis of future potential, our past sacrifices make letting go increasingly difficult, causing further damage.

- **Mental Accounting:** Our minds compartmentalize previous winnings from those still at risk. Past gains on an asset feel separate from its current worth, driving our hesitation to 'cash out' and sacrifice that emotional win, even if a decline will make that initial profit disappear.

These potent factors fuel the disposition effect's detrimental impact on decision-making:

- **Diminished Returns:** The 'high' associated with winning often prevents us from taking our profit at the right time so we can reinvestment in even better opportunities. Conversely, we are reluctant to admit a mistake when our assets are failing, only prolonging corrective action and further eroding our returns.

- **Erosion of a Balanced Portfolio:** The emotional distortion creates bias towards specific holdings, increasing risk and warping diversification principles. Sentiment trumps strategy, leaving a portfolio exposed and potentially fragile.

- **Missed Opportunities:** Fear of realizing losses induces paralysis, making capital inaccessible for new opportunities or nimble shifts in response to market dynamics.

Fortunately, there are strategies for minimizing its impact:

- **Pre-Determined Profit/Loss Points:** Defining these 'triggers' at the time of purchase, while calm and collected, reduces the chance of hesitation caused by later emotional spikes.

- **Forced Diversification:** Periodic portfolio rebalancing limits our over-attachment to specific holdings and helps maintain an asset allocation less vulnerable to psychological distortions.

- **Partnering for Accountability:** Advisors or peers less personally invested in a particular stock can provide much-needed reality checks and offer support in maintaining focus on an overall investment strategy rather than getting fixated on an individual asset's highs and lows.

Questions for Self-Reflection

1. **Observing the Disposition Effect:** Have you witnessed the disposition effect play out in your own investing, or with those you advise? What were the outcomes?

2. **Asset Attachment:** Is there a particular type of asset you're more likely to stubbornly hold onto despite unfavourable conditions? What reasons lie behind that?

3. **Long-Term Goals Over Short-Term Losses:** When making a sale purely to realize a loss, how do you maintain focus on the big picture benefits rather than the temporary discomfort?

XXXVII. THE AFFECT HEURISTIC

Gut Instinct

Maya leaned back in her chair, trying to shake off the tension coursing through her. As CEO of a thriving marketing firm, she'd built her reputation on a laser-sharp ability to translate raw data into winning campaigns. She specialized in target markets, conversion rates and brand alignment, not nebulous feelings or inexplicable hunches. Yet, here she was, agonizing over a decision and leaning towards a choice that defied everything her usual analytics-driven approach stood for.

The deal with EverRise Organics had always been an off-kilter affair. The pitch from their earnest young CEO, Anya, held the promise of disrupting the staid natural beauty market. Ethical sourcing, bold eco-packaging and an online community that Maya's social media analysts deemed 'authentic' – EverRise encapsulated the buzzwords clients paid top dollar for. Yet, on paper, their growth seemed almost too rapid, their financials dangerously skewed towards reinvested profits over stability, and Anya, while passionately articulate, lacked concrete experience in scaling a company this quickly. All red flags.

And still…something kept drawing Maya back in. There was a genuine sense of mission she found stirring, a reminder of the idealistic fervour that propelled her own company's creation. She couldn't discount Anya's charisma either, which mirrored her own 'challenge the norm' spirit. And hadn't Maya's instincts got her this far? This conflict threw her into an uncharacteristic spiral of second-guesses.

In the boardroom, the presentation sparked echoes of that familiar dissonance. Her CFO, Ben, frowned over the balance sheet, muttering, 'A high risk, low reward scenario just doesn't add up'. Her creative director, though visibly jazzed by EverRise's aesthetic, echoed the concern, 'We've made our name with reliability, not flash-in-the-pan trends'. These warnings should have comforted Maya, confirming her initial reservations. Instead, a surge of prickly defensiveness ran up her spine. They just didn't get it – this was about capturing a movement, not ticking boxes on a risk-assessment document.

That evening, she went over the EverRise files again. It was her standard tactic – overwork the data to soothe any niggling anxieties. Each graph and each meticulously footnoted market report should have brought order to the chaos she felt swirling in her head. But then she'd stumble upon a snippet from Anya's blog about transforming her parents' small-town herb farm into the EverRise vision. And there it was – that warmth and idealism she knew firsthand that wasn't always easy to quantify. But was she letting those intangible 'feels' overrule a rational business decision?

The Affect Heuristic

The affect heuristic is a cornerstone concept in understanding human decision-making, especially in how emotions and 'gut feelings' significantly influence our judgments and choices across a spectrum of contexts. This heuristic underscores the interplay between emotion and cognition, illustrating how affective responses can guide our evaluations and decisions, often bypassing more deliberate, analytical thought processes.

Psychologists Daniel Kahneman and Paul Slovic, among others, have extensively documented how affective responses serve as a mental shortcut, enabling individuals to make quick, albeit sometimes flawed, judgments. This heuristic is powered by these factors:

- **Associative Memory:** Human memory is associative, linking new stimuli with past experiences and emotions. When encountering a choice or stimulus, the brain rapidly assesses associated memories and feelings in an attempt to guide the decision-making process with minimal cognitive effort.

- **Evolutionary Adaptation:** From an evolutionary perspective, the affect heuristic is a survival mechanism. Rapid emotional responses to potential threats (e.g., fear in dangerous situations) enabled quick action. In contemporary settings, this mechanism might trigger an emotional response to non-life-threatening stimuli, affecting our decisions in more complex scenarios where a slower, analytical approach might be warranted.

- **Cognitive Load:** In situations of decision overload or complexity, the brain may default to affective responses as a means of simplifying the decision-making process. This can lead to choices that feel right emotionally, even if they lack a solid rational basis.

The affect heuristic influences a wide range of decisions and behaviours:

- **Consumer Behaviour:** Marketing and advertising strategies often exploit the affect heuristic by creating positive emotional associations with products or brands, influencing our purchasing decisions based on feelings rather than product attributes or value.

- **Financial Decision-Making:** Investors may favour investments that elicit positive emotions, such as excitement or optimism, over those supported by rigorous financial analysis. This can lead to biases such as overconfidence or FOMO (fear of missing out), affecting portfolio performance.

- **Social and Political Judgments:** Political campaigns and social movements leverage the affect heuristic by crafting messages that evoke strong emotional responses, which often shapes public opinion and behaviour more effectively than nuanced argumentation.

To counter the influence of the affect heuristic, individuals and organizations can adopt several strategies:

- **Awareness and Education:** Recognizing the role of emotions in decision-making can help individuals identify when their judgments may be unduly influenced by affective responses.

- **Emotional Regulation:** Techniques for managing emotional responses, such as mindfulness or reflective pause before decision-making, can reduce the sway of immediate emotional reactions.

- **Analytical Cross-Checking:** Implementing structured analytical frameworks or checklists for decision-making can provide a counterbalance to affect-driven judgments, ensuring that decisions are grounded in comprehensive analysis.

The affect heuristic illuminates the profound impact of emotions on decision-making, revealing both the heuristic's adaptive value and its potential pitfalls. By understanding and addressing the influence of affective responses, individuals can enhance their decision-making processes, striking a balance between the intuitive power of emotions and the rigour of analytical thought. This balance is crucial for navigating the complexities of the modern world, where decisions often carry significant consequences across personal, professional and societal domains.

Questions for Self-Reflection

1. **Navigating Negative Gut Reactions:** Do you find yourself disliking an idea instantly for reasons you can't fully articulate, leading to discounting of its merits under a fog of vague negativity?

2. **Scrutinizing Positive Gut Reactions:** When facing a positive gut reaction, do you actively push yourself to consider what underlying assumptions or irrelevant positive associations are driving that feeling?

3. **Learning from Impulsive Decisions:** Have you ever regretted acting impulsively on a 'can't miss' instinct, when you face the consequences or the missed opportunities later on?

4. **Valuing Diverse Perspectives:** Are you creating space for critical feedback and a diversity of views to counterbalance your initial 'feels', or do you surround yourself with agreeable figures that fuel your confirmation bias?

5. **Intuition vs Evidence in Performance Reviews:** In performance reviews, do you praise people based on your gut impression or on demonstrable behaviours and documented goals that have been achieved or missed?

XXXVIII. REGRET AVERSION

The Hesitant Investor

In the bustling world of finance, Eleanor, a prudent investment manager, found herself at a crossroads with one of her long-held tech stocks: TechGen. Over the past year, TechGen's performance had been lacklustre, trailing behind its industry peers. The broader market was bullish, yet TechGen seemed stuck in a quagmire of developmental delays and competitive pressures. Eleanor's initial investment thesis, which banked on TechGen's innovative product lineup to drive growth, was now under scrutiny.

Eleanor's dilemma was not just about whether to hold or sell TechGen; it was deeply rooted in her aversion to regret. She was haunted by a previous decision where she had sold a different stock too early, only to watch its value soar months later – a mistake that had cost her significantly. This experience had instilled a deep fear in her of making another bad decision and potentially missing out on gains if TechGen's fortunes were to turn around after she sold.

Despite the mounting evidence that it might be time to divest and reallocate her investment to more promising opportunities, Eleanor hesitated. Her analysis was thorough, yet she found herself paralyzed, unable to make the decisive move. This hesitation was emblematic of regret aversion – fearing the emotional pain of regret more than the financial loss itself.

As weeks turned into months, TechGen's situation did not improve. Eleanor's portfolio began to feel the weight of her indecision, underperforming against benchmarks that included more agile investors who had divested from TechGen early on. It was a sobering lesson for Eleanor, underscoring the cost of inaction and the grip that fear of regret can have on investment decisions.

This experience became a pivotal learning moment for Eleanor, prompting her to reevaluate her investment strategy and decision-making process. She recognized the need to balance her analytical rigour with emotional resilience, understanding that the fear of regret should not overshadow the fundamentals of sound investment practice.

Regret Aversion

Regret aversion, a psychological phenomenon that significantly influences investment behaviour, explains the natural human tendency to anticipate regret over making an unfavourable decision and, consequently, to take or avoid actions to prevent this emotional discomfort. This behaviour is particularly evident in the realm of investing, where decisions are often fraught with uncertainty and the potential for loss.

At its core, regret aversion is rooted in our emotional response to the possibility of making a decision that leads to a poor outcome, especially when an alternative choice could have been made. In the context of investing, this can manifest in several ways. For instance, an investor might be hesitant to sell an underperforming asset due to the fear that, once sold, the asset's value might increase, leading to regret. Similarly, an investor might avoid taking on a potentially lucrative investment opportunity due to the fear that it will perform poorly and they will regret making the investment in the first place.

The implications of regret aversion on investment strategies are profound. Investors may exhibit overly conservative behaviour, preferring to stick with safer, lower-yield investments rather than exploring options that, while riskier, could offer higher returns. This can lead to a portfolio that is under-diversified. Moreover, regret aversion can contribute to the disposition effect, where investors are too quick to sell winning investments to lock in gains and avoid the regret of a potential downturn, while simultaneously holding onto losing investments in the hope they will rebound, to avoid the regret of realizing a loss.

To mitigate the impact of regret aversion, investors can adopt several strategies:

- **Acknowledge the Role of Emotions:** By recognizing the influence of regret aversion, investors can take steps to ensure their investment choices are driven by rational analysis rather than emotional responses.
- **Outlining a Clear Investment Plan and Goals:** Developing a well-thought-out investment plan and setting clear goals can help investors stay focused on their long-term objectives, reducing the temptation to make impulsive decisions based on short-term market movements or the fear of regret. Regularly reviewing and adjusting one's investment portfolio in line with these goals can help investors maintain an objective perspective.

- **Diversification:** This is another key strategy for mitigating regret aversion. By spreading investments across a variety of asset classes, sectors and geographies, investors can reduce the risk of significant losses from a single investment, thereby minimizing the potential for regret.

In conclusion, regret aversion is a powerful psychological force that can significantly influence investment behaviour, often leading to overly conservative investment strategies and the potential underperformance of a portfolio. By understanding and acknowledging the impact of regret aversion, investors can take proactive steps to ensure their decisions are guided by rational analysis and aligned with their long-term financial goals.

Questions for Self-Reflection

1. **The Impact of Regret Aversion:** Have you ever held onto an investment longer than you should have because you feared regretting a decision to sell? Reflect on the outcome and consider how the fear of regret influenced your decision-making process.

2. **Decision Paralysis:** Think about a time when you missed out on an investment opportunity because you were afraid of making the wrong decision. How did this aversion to potential regret affect your portfolio in the long run?

3. **Mitigating Regret Aversion:** Consider how you can incorporate mechanisms to mitigate the influence of regret aversion in your investment strategy. Could setting more

rigorous investment criteria or establishing predefined exit strategies for your investments help reduce the impact of emotional biases on your decisions?

4. **Balancing Emotion and Analysis:** Reflect on the balance between emotional intuition and analytical decision-making in your investment process. How can you ensure that your investment decisions are driven by data and analysis rather than the fear of regret?

5. **Learning and Growth:** Think about the role of learning and growth in overcoming regret aversion. How can past investment experiences, both positive and negative, inform your future investment decisions without leading to paralysis by analysis?

PART 3

SOCIAL BIASES

XXXIX. THE HALO EFFECT

The Dazzle of Reputation

From her earliest days in graduate school, Sarah held a deep-seated reverence for Dr. Katherine Evans. While other students pinned posters of celebrities to their dorm walls, Sarah's idols were pioneering scientists, and Dr. Evans occupied a hallowed spot among them. To Sarah, she wasn't merely a prominent environmental scientist; she embodied a vital combination of intellectual rigour, persuasive communication and an unwavering commitment to driving real-world impact. This potent trio ignited Sarah's own ambitions.

Then came the email Sarah never dared to dream of: an invitation to collaborate on a project spearheaded by Dr. Evans herself. An electrifying surge of excitement and self-doubt ran through Sarah as she accepted without hesitation. This was more than a career milestone; it was a chance to learn from the best and to prove herself worthy of her place in the field.

Initially, Sarah was dazzled by Dr. Evans' sharp intellect and strategic thinking. Their brainstorming sessions crackled with energy. Witnessing her idol navigate the labyrinthine world of grant proposals and policymaking filled Sarah with a potent mixture of awe and a desire to make her own contributions count.

Dr. Evans advocated for ambitious, rapid-scale deployment of a nascent renewable energy technology. In principle, Sarah championed the urgency. Yet, her in-depth knowledge of local ecosystems and wildlife migration corridors raised alarm bells. The sheer velocity of Dr. Evans' vision could bring unintended environmental costs. This conflict ate away at Sarah; questioning a luminary in her field felt akin to heresy. Could she, a less experienced researcher, possibly be seeing flaws that were invisible to the brilliant Dr. Evans?

As the project progressed, Sarah began noticing a pattern. During planning sessions, Dr. Evans seemed captivated by streamlined presentations and bold statements over detailed evidence. When others expressed concerns about logistical delays or budget overruns, Dr. Evans would brush them aside, focusing on the grand vision with unwavering optimism. In team discussions, she effortlessly deflected doubts with an easy laugh, her charisma diffusing any lingering worries.

A pivotal moment occurred in a boardroom meeting with potential project funders. Citing data that Sarah knew to be preliminary, Dr. Evans made sweeping pronouncements about the technology's groundbreaking potential. Then, she advocated for accelerating the timeline without factoring in environmental reviews. When a board member tentatively raised the issue of those reviews, Dr. Evans painted them as bureaucratic hurdles that were delaying urgent climate action.

Sarah's sense of disquiet morphed into a full-blown internal crisis. Her research screamed caution, and her ethical compass felt thrown off-kilter. Yet, confronting Dr. Evans directly felt terrifying. What if she was wrong? The fallout from challenging someone with Dr. Evans' influence could torpedo Sarah's entire career.

Torn and restless, Sarah sought advice from a seasoned mentor outside the project. They listened intently, offering neither immediate praise nor judgment. Instead, they focused on teasing apart Sarah's feelings. It was not just fear that made her reluctant, but a shattering realization: her halo-tinted perceptions of Dr. Evans had clouded her judgment. The mentor guided Sarah to focus on the heart of the matter: not Dr. Evans' reputation, but facts, meticulous research and responsible execution.

It took immense courage, but Sarah voiced her concerns to Dr. Evans. To her surprise, the encounter did not result in animosity. Instead, a more collaborative conversation ensued where they reassessed the timeline and identified areas for deeper investigation. This experience didn't shatter Sarah's respect for Dr. Evans, but it redefined it, grounding it in a newfound respect for critical thinking even when challenging those she admired.

The Halo Effect

Sarah's experience embodies the powerful and often unnoticed influence of the halo effect. This cognitive bias operates on a deceptively simple principle: our overall favourable impression of a person, brand or concept spills over, unconsciously shaping how we judge their specific traits, capabilities and actions. Essentially, if we like one thing about them, we unconsciously inflate our perceptions of other, even unrelated, aspects.

The 'halo' can be formed by various factors:

- **Attractiveness:** Studies consistently show that physically attractive individuals are often attributed other positive qualities – higher intelligence, trustworthiness and competence, for example – a bias deeply rooted in cultural messaging and evolutionarily hardwired preferences.

- **Fame and Reputation:** People or companies with established success can generate such a glowing halo that critical assessment dims. We assume that those who earn accolades must be outstanding in every respect.
- **Similarity:** An underlying feeling of kinship can emerge if we identify with someone's background, personality or shared values. This connection generates a sense of trust, sometimes obscuring a fair appraisal of their ideas or conduct.
- **First Impressions:** Our initial encounters are potent in terms of shaping our perceptions. A confident demeanour, charisma or simply liking someone on a personal level creates a positive 'anchor' that warps our subsequent judgments.

The halo effect isn't solely negative. It plays a key role in helping us to quickly navigate our complex social world, influencing trust and initial rapport. However, the dangers lie in the consequences of unchallenged halos:

- **Poor Decision-Making:** From hiring less qualified but charming candidates to overpaying for products simply because of the brand name, we let positive associations trump clear evaluation.
- **Lack of Critical Assessment:** When a halo is in place, we tend to minimize dissenting voices or contrary evidence,

which fosters an environment hostile to thoughtful critique or course correction.
- **Missed Flaws:** We may unintentionally overlook shortcomings, especially ones that go against the shiny image generated by the halo. This can be damaging in relationships, business ventures and even in the case of trends driven by celebrity endorsements.

Understanding the halo effect is vital for critical thinking. The initial step is awareness of its existence, as it often works through an almost subconscious shortcut in our mental processing.

Questions for Self-Reflection

1. **Identifying Your Halos:** Are there individuals in your life whose opinions carry substantial weight due to their accomplishments or titles?

2. **The Dazzle Factor:** Can you recall instances where a company's reputation or the sheer charisma of a spokesperson affected your judgment of their offerings?

3. **Challenging Assumptions:** When someone you admire puts forth an idea, how open are you to recognizing its potential flaws?

4. **Separating Fact from Perception:** How can you differentiate your overall impression of an individual from a neutral assessment of their specific statements or actions?

5. **Trusting Your Instincts:** If a small, uneasy feeling persists about someone with a 'halo', how can you investigate that without becoming cynical or automatically dismissive

XL. HERD MENTALITY

The Echo of the Crowd

Known for his scrupulous research and independent judgment, Michael had navigated the treacherous waters of the stock market with unparalleled acumen. His career was a testament to the power of analytical rigour over the whims of market sentiment, earning him both respect and admiration from his peers.

However, the emergence of a new technology sector, heralded as the next frontier in innovation, presented an unprecedented challenge to Michael's principles. The sector's stocks began to soar, fuelled by a relentless stream of media hype and bullish investor sentiment. The market buzz was inescapable, with every report and every analysis pointing towards the same conclusion: the sector was on the brink of revolutionizing the world, and those who failed to invest would be left in its wake.

As Michael observed the frenzy from the sidelines, he felt the weight of doubt for the first time in his career. His colleagues, many of whom he had regarded as rational and discerning investors, were swept up in the euphoria, reallocating vast sums into the burgeoning sector. The trading floors were humming with tales of overnight fortunes made from skyrocketing stocks, and the air was thick with anticipation of even greater gains.

The collective conviction of the market was intoxicating. Despite his reservations, Michael found himself drawn to the idea of being part of what was being heralded as an historic financial opportunity. The fear of missing out on such a monumental wave of growth gnawed at him, eroding his resolve. The pressure to conform, to not be left behind as the only sceptic in a sea of believers, was immense.

Yielding to the siren call of the crowd, Michael made the decision to invest a significant portion of his portfolio into the sector. It was a move that went against every instinct he had honed over his years on the trading floor, but the allure of potential profits and the fear of being the outlier when there was market consensus proved too strong to resist.

However, as the initial excitement began to wane, reality set in. The sector's growth, while impressive, was not the inexorable march to dominance that had been predicted. Technological challenges, regulatory hurdles and slower-than-expected consumer adoption began to temper the initial optimism. The market corrected sharply, and the sector's stocks plummeted, leaving Michael and countless others facing significant losses.

This experience was a sobering reminder of the potent effect of herd mentality on investment decisions. Michael had allowed the fear of missing out, an overreliance on the perceived wisdom of the crowd and the social influence of collective sentiment to cloud his judgment.

In the aftermath, Michael reflected on the lessons learned from this ordeal. Determined to regain his footing, he committed to reaffirming his dedication to thorough research, independent thinking and caution, recognizing that true success in investing comes not from following the crowd but from navigating the market with discernment and resilience.

This experience underscored the importance of vigilance against the psychological biases that can distort our investment decisions. For Michael, and for investors everywhere, it served as a reminder that in the face of market mania, our greatest asset is the ability to think critically and act independently.

Herd Mentality

Herd Mentality, or Herding Bias, particularly within the context of financial markets, represents a complex interplay of psychological tendencies, social dynamics and economic implications. It goes beyond mere mimicry of actions, delving into the depths of human behaviour and its impact on market efficiency, asset valuation and the cyclical nature of booms and busts.

At its core, herd mentality is rooted in evolutionary psychology. Early humans who stuck with the group were more likely to survive threats; thus, modern humans have inherited a deep-seated propensity to follow the crowd, especially under conditions of uncertainty or stress. In financial markets, this instinct manifests itself when investors, faced with complex decisions and unpredictable outcomes, look to the behaviour of others as a heuristic or shortcut for action.

Herd mentality is also significantly influenced by social proof, a term coined by psychologist Robert Cialdini, and a concept we'll explore in the next chapter. It describes how individuals look to the behaviour of others to guide their own actions in situations where the correct behaviour is uncertain. In investment contexts, social proof can lead to information cascades, where investors ignore their private information in favour of imitating others' actions, under the assumption that these actions are informed by superior knowledge.

Fear of missing out, or FOMO, driven by an emotional response to potential regret and loss, is also part of the herd mentality, and a powerful motivator of financial decision-making. The rapid dissemination of information through digital media amplifies this effect, as investors are constantly bombarded with stories of overnight success and tales of those who 'got in early' on a lucrative investment. The fear of missing out on these opportunities can override rational analysis, leading investors to make decisions based on emotion rather than fundamentals.

Herd mentality is also reinforced by a belief in the collective wisdom of the market, a concept that suggests the aggregate decisions of market participants can lead to optimal outcomes. While there is merit to this idea, especially in the context of efficient market hypothesis, it can become problematic when the crowd's actions are based more on sentiment than on solid financial analysis. The assumption that a large number of investors cannot be wrong about an investment can lead to bubbles and subsequent crashes when the underlying economic realities are finally acknowledged.

Herd mentality can have profound implications for market efficiency and asset pricing. It can contribute to the formation of asset bubbles, where prices are driven to unsustainable levels by collective enthusiasm rather than intrinsic value. Similarly, it can exacerbate market downturns, as panic selling leads to rapid declines in asset prices. Understanding herd mentality is crucial for regulators and policymakers in designing mechanisms to mitigate systemic risk and for investors in developing strategies to navigate volatile markets.

- **Diversification:** By spreading investments across various asset classes, sectors and geographies, investors can reduce the impact of herding-induced market movements on their portfolios.

- **Contrarian Investing:** Adopting a contrarian approach involves taking positions that are opposite to the prevailing market sentiment, allowing you to capitalize on corrections if the market readjusts.

- **Continuous Education and Awareness:** Staying informed about the psychological biases that influence investment decisions can help investors recognize when their actions might be driven by herd mentality rather than independent analysis.

Herd mentality underscores the complexity of financial markets, where human psychology plays a significant role in shaping economic outcomes. By understanding the roots and ramifications of this bias, investors can better navigate the challenges of investment decision-making, balancing the wisdom of the crowd with individual analysis.

Questions for Self-Reflection

1. **Following the Crowd:** Can you recall a time when you went along with a decision or action primarily because others were doing it, even if you had reservations?

2. **Fear of Missing Out (FOMO):** Do you ever feel pressure to participate in popular trends or activities due to a fear of being left behind or excluded?

3. **Unquestioned Confidence:** Have you ever encountered someone whose strong conviction in an idea made you doubt your own judgment, even if your intuition told you otherwise?

4. **Challenging the Norm:** How comfortable are you questioning common group views or voicing a dissenting opinion, even if it feels socially risky?

5. **Independent Thinking:** What strategies do you have to cultivate independent thinking and avoid blindly following the majority?

XLI. SOCIAL PROOF

The Lure of Popularity

Maddie, a marketing director for a mid-sized cosmetics brand, faced the task of revitalizing their established but stagnating 'Revive' skincare serum. While well-respected by loyal customers and generally effective, the line simply wasn't capturing the imagination of new target audiences. They needed a spark, something bold to cut through the onslaught of flashier, social media-savvy launches from competitors.

One morning, Maddie's brainstorming session with her team was upended. A team member had excitedly stumbled upon a skincare guru taking the internet by storm. 'Her name is Anya', the team member gushed. 'She's young, super stylish and authentic – her followers swear by everything she recommends!' Anya's videos showcased routines filled with products, each bestowed with playful hashtags and glowing declarations about their supposed transformative powers.

Intrigued, Maddie went down the rabbit hole of Anya's content. It wasn't just the production quality; Anya possessed an engaging blend of self-deprecating humour and aspirational glamour. While occasionally mentioning sponsorships, most products seemed like genuine must-haves that she had discovered on her own. Anya's glowing declarations about a European luxury serum caught Maddie's attention. With its sleek packaging and sky-high price, it promised visible age-defying effects through an exclusive blend of ingredients.

While not a direct rival to 'Revive' due to the significant price difference, Maddie's initial excitement about the product dimmed when she researched the ingredients. She couldn't deny the serum's formulation was potent, with the potential to yield results, but it was similar to what some of her company's existing lines already promised at a fraction of the cost. It wasn't a miracle solution to ageing. Still, a wave of unease settled in. Should she dismiss a product this popular so readily? Maddie couldn't shake the feeling of being behind the curve – out of touch with what real consumers desired.

Scrolling through the serum's online reviews and countless 'selfies' posted by enthusiastic users, Maddie hesitated. Yes, some positive comments likely stemmed from paid promotion or brand allegiance, regardless of results. Yet, the sheer volume of praise felt undeniable. Maddie, usually confident in her ability to separate hype from value, felt conflicted. She understood the concept of social proof, but her instincts told her this went beyond targeted advertisements; Anya's followers formed a genuine community, sharing skincare struggles and fiercely championing products that made them feel beautiful and confident.

Could 'Revive' generate such passion? The team began dissecting this phenomenon. What if it wasn't about the ingredients alone, but a holistic image of unattainable yet relatable luxury? Anya's personal stories made followers feel a part of her beauty journey. 'Revive' had never emphasized this aspirational component. Maybe an edgy rebranding and a fresh messaging style focused on transformation was needed. After all, the serum delivered results; they simply had not emphasized them convincingly enough. Yet, doubt lingered. Were they about to drastically revise their strategy based on a belief in the power of hype rather than proven results?

Anya's next 'skincare secrets revealed' tutorial featured three new products Maddie barely recognized. Was this a potential opportunity for 'Revive' or merely more proof that relying on the fleeting attention of influencers for long-term revitalization was a losing game? The choice Maddie faced wasn't simply about marketing a serum; it was battling a deeply human inclination to trust the wisdom of the crowd versus forging a strong independent brand identity.

Social Proof

Maddie's experience spotlights the multifaceted and influential nature of social proof. It lies at the heart of marketing and fashion trends and often shapes our decision-making more profoundly than we care to admit. At its core, social proof stems from our evolutionarily hardwired tendency to look to others for cues on how to act. In uncertain or complex situations, observing the choices of our peers and wider society feels like a shortcut to making the 'right' decisions.

This reliance on social signals served us well in prehistoric times when imitating group behaviour could be vital to survival. While we have adapted some elements – we're not likely to blindly copy someone jumping off a cliff! – the underlying psychological power remains, especially when cleverly orchestrated to create powerful consumer desires. Here's why it's so challenging to counteract:

- **Uncertainty Bypass:** Faced with endless product options or unfamiliar circumstances, the sheer quantity of people praising something is alluring. It promises acceptance, belonging and the satisfaction of having chosen 'wisely'.

- **Safety in Numbers:** Seeing many others engage in a behaviour triggers an assumption that it mustn't be harmful. Even in areas where we hold expertise, we can second-guess ourselves when faced with overwhelming social consensus that contradicts our perspective.
- **The Illusion of Expertise:** When those sharing positive endorsements appear knowledgeable or hold real (or manufactured) authority, we place even greater weight on their views.
- **Aspirational Influence:** Social proof fuels desire. Products and trends connected to celebrity lifestyles, youth subcultures or exclusive access generate a 'if they have it, I want it' mentality, regardless of true need.
- **FOMO Factor:** Social media amplifies the fear of missing out. Observing trends explode online triggers anxieties about being excluded if we don't participate. This sense of urgency bypasses logical and cost-benefit analysis.

While social proof shouldn't be dismissed entirely – sometimes the crowd *is* onto worthwhile offerings – it leads to several concerning implications if left unchecked:

- **Herd Mentality:** When the 'herd' dictates what's acceptable, it can undermine independent judgment and a questioning approach. This stifles innovation and exploration outside of trending ideas.

- **Manipulation and Fakes:** Astute marketers and less scrupulous individuals skilfully manufacture viral buzz. Paid 'influencers' stage reviews and bot-generated hype can distort realities about efficacy and demand.
- **Echo Chambers:** Online algorithms curate our environments, feeding us more of what we already interact with. This fuels the illusion of social proof for even dubious products, limiting exposure to critical or varied perspectives.

Recognizing the pull of social proof isn't about turning into a relentless cynic. Rather, it's a call to cultivate awareness of how these unconscious desires can be exploited. We need strategies to move beyond an 'it must be great because it's everywhere' attitude and foster our own informed decision-making skills.

Questions for Self-Reflection

1. **Popularity vs Utility:** When making professional choices, how do you ensure a focus on objectively verifiable performance rather than popularity?

2. **The Cost of Hype:** Are there areas of your decision-making where a rush to be seen as 'in-the-know' or capitalizing on viral trends may overshadow more stable, long-term strategies?

3. **Authentic Representation:** Is there a discrepancy between the social proof surrounding a product, service or trend and its observable benefits within your unique context?

4. **Fact vs Perception:** Is your team skilled at differentiating between the power of social proof as a marketing tool versus allowing it to influence their own decision-making?

5. **Independent Judgment:** How can you foster a culture where the desire to follow popular trends is balanced against critical evaluations born from genuine expertise?

XLII. IN-GROUP FAVOURITISM

The Rival Bake Sales

Picture two neighbourhood groups: the Maple Street Crew and the Oak Avenue Bunch. Their paths cross at bake sales, PTA meetings and the occasional awkward run-in at the dog park. There's a veneer of friendly politeness, but a subtle competitiveness simmers beneath the surface. For years, each group has held bake sales for good causes, though whispers always circulate about who raised the most funds.

For Sarah, a Maple Street resident since childhood, the bake sale isn't just about delicious treats. It's about community, the camaraderie of setting up with neighbours as the sun peeks over the rooftops. Yet, as the years go by, Sarah feels something is changing within her. With every customer that chooses their cookies over Oak Avenue's muffins, there's a small thrill of triumph that goes beyond supporting the charity. When a customer hesitates before browsing the Oak Avenue stall, Sarah catches herself smugly hoping they'll turn back towards the familiar faces of Maple Street.

Later, while enjoying a lemonade, a display of blueberry muffins on Oak Avenue's table grabs Sarah's attention. They look homemade and delicious. Yet, she hesitates to go and try one. She finds herself thinking: 'Those probably aren't that good anyway. Our chocolate chip cookies have always been the best'. She justifies passing them by, secretly wondering if her treats might magically taste sweeter simply because fellow Maple Street residents baked them.

In-Group Favouritism

At first glance, Sarah's experience seems trivial. After all, it's only muffins. But those seemingly minor behaviours stem from a potent psychological phenomenon: in-group favouritism. Let's unpack what is going on beneath the surface:

- **The Power of Categorization:** Humans have a fundamental need to belong. Even arbitrary divisions like living on a certain street can become sources of identity and group membership. Simply perceiving 'Maple Street' as her in-group sets the stage for favouritism to unconsciously emerge in Sarah.

- **Identity Boost:** Part of self-esteem comes from the groups we belong to. Favouritism towards these groups reinforces a positive self-image. Choosing 'her' baked goods and celebrating their superiority affirms her personal association with the winning side.

- **Competition as Fuel:** While friendly on the surface, the competitive aspect amplifies the us vs them dynamic. Success becomes defined not only by how well your group does but by how you fare in comparison to the out-group.

- **Confirmation Bias at Play:** Once bias sets in, the mind subtly seeks ways to justify it. Negative characteristics (the questionable freshness of those blueberry muffins) might get exaggerated when associated with the out-group, while any imperfections within the in-group are downplayed or overlooked.

- **Emotional Investment:** With each shared success, the feeling of 'we built this' grows. Sarah didn't bake every single cookie, but contributing to the Maple Street table creates a connection with the team effort and boosts her emotional stake in its success.

Sarah's tale illustrates a mild case of in-group favouritism that happens unconsciously and mostly expresses itself in seemingly harmless preferences. But the same underlying principles influence attitudes and behaviours in much larger arenas:

- **Politics:** When political parties become our 'team', differing views aren't simply disagreements. They threaten our identity, making compromise difficult and fuelling societal divide.

- **Work and Organizations:** In-groups can emerge at work, hindering cross-department collaboration, making external partnerships less appealing and creating blind spots that harm the organization.

- **Online Communities:** Social media and niche interest groups, while providing connection, can breed a digital version of in-group bias. Shared beliefs get reinforced within this 'echo chamber', and alternative viewpoints are often painted in a negative light.

- **Fandoms and Cultural Tribes:** Intense fandoms can form fervent in-groups where favouring a certain team, artist or lifestyle can easily slide into disparaging any perceived competitors or 'outsiders'.

Our tendency to develop in-group preferences has deep evolutionary origins. In ancient times, forming quick attachments and trust within your tribe often determined survival. Our 21st century societies are different, yet that instinctive 'us vs them' wiring persists. While not inherently wrong (community bonding has its benefits), unchecked in-group favouritism in today's complex, interconnected world creates problems:

- **Prejudice and Discrimination:** Favouritism can become a gateway to outright prejudice. Subtle preferences easily get inflated, justifying negative stereotypes and harmful behaviours towards 'others'.

- **Missed Connections:** Judging someone by a group label might blind us to the talent, skills and valuable perspectives those outside our circle might offer.

- **Entrenched Conflict:** Exaggerated in-group loyalty leads to demonizing the out-group, making negotiation difficult and potentially leading to escalation of conflict.

- **Echo Chambers and Lost Opportunities:** Seeking comfort in groups of like-minded individuals makes us less likely to challenge our own biases or hear alternative views, leading to missed opportunities for personal and societal growth.

A fascinating aspect of in-group favouritism lies in how easily in-groups are created. In studies dubbed 'minimal group' experiments, researchers separated participants using the most arbitrary criteria ('Do you tend to overestimate or underestimate the number of dots on a screen?'). Despite these meaningless groupings, the newly formed 'teams' quickly displayed signs of favouritism – rating their in-group members higher and allocating them more resources, for instance.

Why does this matter? It indicates that categorization alone triggers 'us vs them' thinking. Now, imagine those same psychological processes occurring in environments where they might have tangible impacts: in the workplace during hiring decisions, in social groups with deeply embedded cultural differences or within nations shaped by long-standing territorial divides.

Realizing in-group favouritism is a normal human impulse is the first step. It's not cause for guilt but for increased self-awareness. Here are some ways to mitigate its harm:

- **Challenging the Labels:** Take note of the automatic categorizations your mind engages in. Instead of dwelling on differences, seek common ground and shared humanity across perceived divides.

- **Focusing on Individuals:** Don't let group stereotypes eclipse the unique contributions of individual members, whether they belong to your in-group or an out-group.

- **Cultivating Humility and Empathy:** Remind yourself that your own view may be limited. Actively seek to understand the experiences and perspectives of those from different backgrounds and groups.

- **Embracing Healthy Competition:** Keep rivalry in perspective. Celebrate wins without dehumanizing your 'opponents'. There's a difference between, 'We did great!' and, 'We did great because they're less than us'.

- **Creating Superordinate Goals:** Cooperation becomes easier when an important shared goal requires diverse groups to work together. This shifts the focus from competition to a shared interest in succeeding together.

Questions for Self-Reflection

Recognizing group dynamics like those Sarah experienced takes honesty and reflection. Consider these questions for self-exploration:

1. **A Sense of Belonging:** Where do you feel a sense of 'us'? List groups you strongly identify with (based around work teams, cultural identity, hobbies, etc.). Is your loyalty to these groups serving you well, or could it be harmful?

2. **Competition Increases Favouritism:** Does competition amplify your bias against 'others'? Are you likely to treat those outside your group less favourably when there's something at stake?

3. **Negative Thoughts About 'Others':** When feeling negatively about an out-group, do you challenge those thoughts? Are your reasons based on direct experiences or assumptions absorbed from being in your group?

4. **Celebrating Without Dismissing:** Can you applaud your in-group's wins without needing to downplay someone else's achievements or effort?

5. **Being a Group Ambassador:** When interacting with those outside your group, do you represent your in-group as one of respect and openness? Do you avoid behaviours or language that confirm negative stereotypes about your group in the eyes of others?

XLIII. OPTIMISM BIAS

The Story of Sunny Sam

Sam isn't just an optimist; he's the definition of it. Every cloud in his world has a conspicuously sparkly lining. At first, his unwavering positivity in the office was infectious. When Monday mornings were met with groans, Sam's chipper, 'This week is gonna be epic!' could turn grumbles into reluctant smiles. Yet, with each particularly messy spreadsheet and each painfully long team meeting, his sunny cheer started to feel faintly out of tune with reality.

The Bright Future Innovations project was one of those messy endeavours. Ambitious to a fault, it involved coordinating with multiple contractors, a demanding timeline and the pressure of securing critical funding that relied on its success. Sam, naturally, was ablaze with excitement and firm confidence. He swept aside raised eyebrows and cautious inquiries from his colleagues. 'Focus on the big picture, folks! Obstacles are merely bumps in the road!' he'd preach, his enthusiasm both relentless and undeniably sincere.

Sam wasn't delusional or oblivious to problems. His dedication was genuine and he worked extra hours to keep things on track. He just always visualized the finish line in his mind's eye, picturing applause and success, while the detailed plan on how to get there was fuzzier around the edges. When a key technical element proved trickier than anticipated, Sam shrugged it off. 'The universe provides!' he'd say, only half-jokingly, revealing his unwavering belief that setbacks would always somehow miraculously resolve themselves.

Sarah, a meticulous analyst on the team, felt a mounting frustration. With every budget overrun and delayed milestone, Sam's positivity seemed less inspiring and more like a refusal to face reality. She longed to inject some data-driven pragmatism into the mix but found it difficult to pierce the bubble of Sam's rosy projections. One particularly frustrating delay led to a missed deadline for an important investor presentation. In the tense aftermath, Sarah finally cracked. 'Your blind optimism is damaging the project, Sam!' she blurted out.

The accusation hurt. Sam felt his relentless good vibes fuelled motivation when deadlines loomed. He believed in his team and their potential, and most importantly, he believed in himself. Yes, things weren't going perfectly, but wasn't positivity what would ultimately turn everything around? It stung to be labelled part of the problem rather than part of a much-needed solution.

He retreated temporarily into his bubble, writing off Sarah's concerns as the grumblings of an inherent pessimist who couldn't grasp the power of unwavering faith. Then, as the project stalled further, an undeniable shift began to happen within Sam. One evening, staring down at a spreadsheet that simply wouldn't cooperate, he felt a creeping realization. Had he become so preoccupied with the end goal that he'd been undervaluing the complexities along the way?

Optimism Bias

Sam's experience highlights something inherent to the human condition: optimism bias, or what scientists sometimes call unrealistic optimism. In simple terms, it describes our tendency to overestimate the probability that we'll experience positive outcomes (winning that grant, launching a successful product) and underestimate the likelihood of negative events (blowing our budget, experiencing delays). In this way, we all wear slightly rose-tinted glasses, believing the future holds far better things for us than statistical probability, or plain old common sense, might suggest.

Optimism bias likely has evolutionary roots. If our ancient ancestors walked fearfully through the world, assuming a tiger waited behind every bush, they were less likely to venture out, explore and potentially discover resources vital for survival. A touch of happy delusion might have spurred necessary risk-taking. There are various contemporary theories as to why this bias endures:

- **Self-Enhancement:** Our self-esteem gets a boost via optimism as it's founded in a belief that we're more capable and luckier than the average person.

- **The Illusion of Control:** Optimism often comes with a sense that we can directly influence outcomes. Even when events are truly out of our hands, this creates a feeling of mastery over uncertainty.

- **Filtering Experiences:** If things generally work out in the end, we naturally remember (and exaggerate) past successes to reinforce that we're on the right track, downplaying mishaps as aberrations.

Optimism bias is neither wholly virtuous nor wholly villainous. Let's consider its benefits and downsides.

Benefits:

- **Motivation and Effort:** Believing in eventual success fosters a can-do attitude. An optimistic mindset fuels hard work, even when obstacles appear.

- **Mental and Physical Health:** Research suggests a potential link between positive outlook and stronger immune function, resilience against stress and even a longer lifespan.

- **Interpersonal Relations:** Optimists tend to be well-liked. Their cheerfulness is often contagious, enhancing their social connections and support system.

Downsides:

- **Recklessness and Poor Planning:** Focusing exclusively on the potential for triumph blinds us to very real risks. Underestimating problems can lead to impulsive and even dangerous decisions that lack adequate planning.

- **Disappointment and Setbacks:** When life inevitably throws curveballs, extreme optimism leaves us unprepared and can cause intense disappointment or a disillusionment that's hard to shake off.

- **Undermining Teamwork:** Unrelenting positivity that shuts down concerns from more pragmatic colleagues can sabotage a project or erode relationships.

With Bright Future Innovations teetering on the edge, Sam grappled with Sarah's feedback. In an honest moment, he realized it wasn't pessimism but rather a desperate plea for calculated optimism – belief in success mixed with an openness to anticipate and proactively resolve difficulties. It was realism she craved, not negativity.

This awareness ignited a change in Sam. His boundless enthusiasm didn't disappear, but it matured. He began holding 'positive brainstorming' sessions with the team, encouraging them to identify potential problems to mitigate as well as envision their eventual success. Sam realized that his unwavering optimism was valuable only when paired with an acceptance of the inevitable hurdles along the way.

Slowly, a balance emerged. Bright Future Innovations was still challenging, but plans became more detailed, with contingency options. Team communication increased. It turned out Sarah was a wealth of knowledge he'd previously dismissed, her meticulous reports revealing critical details he often overlooked in his rush towards the big picture. Sam was changing, not into a pessimist but into a pragmatist armed with the most powerful weapon of all – hope.

Questions for Self-Reflection

Recognizing this bias helps us channel optimism while avoiding its traps. Consider these questions:

1. **Your Success Soundtrack:** When picturing goals, are you focused on the triumphant conclusion rather than the nitty-gritty struggle to get there?

2. **Problem Blindness:** Do you downplay warnings, assuming the power of positive thought will conquer all? Do you frame setbacks as minor inconveniences rather than opportunities for course-correction?

3. **Positive Spin vs Denial:** When challenges arise, do you acknowledge them or do you deflect the conversation towards potential future rewards?

4. **Responding to Doubt:** Is your first reaction defensive when someone expresses doubts? Do you consider diverse viewpoints on their own terms or dismiss them as 'negativity'?

5. **Positivity as an Unmovable Force:** Can you adapt when plans get messy? Does a forced change in direction shake your underlying belief in potential success?

XLIV. REACTANCE

Amelia's Rebellious Streak

Amelia had always cherished her sense of independence. Whether choosing her dramatically mismatched outfits as a child or her slightly unconventional college major, she enjoyed doing things her way. Yet, as she transitioned into her first serious job, something began to shift. Intimidated by office hierarchies and corporate-approved slogans, Amelia felt a strange, defiant impulse surge within her.

One afternoon, an email landed in her inbox: 'All-Staff Wellness Workshop' the title proclaimed in an overly cheerful font. The description promised transformative mindfulness techniques and healthy snack options. Amelia felt her shoulders tense and a wave of irrational annoyance ripple through her. Logically, she knew a session focused on stress management sounded perfectly harmless, even beneficial. Yet, there was something in the way it was packaged — the mandatory nature of it, the forced enthusiasm projected in the wording — that made her instinctively want to roll her eyes and skip the whole thing.

'Don't tell me how to relax', she muttered under her breath as she deleted the email with a sense of defiance that surprised even herself. It wasn't about the mindfulness itself; it was about having these self-help activities pushed on her from above. It was about losing her decision-making power over how she managed her own well-being.

Over the next few weeks, Amelia noticed this defiance wasn't limited to wellness workshops. A suggestion from her well-meaning manager to organize her files differently ignited a flicker of resistance. An 'encouraged' donation for a team-building charity pot rubbed her the wrong way. Even a well-intentioned team happy hour became something she only begrudgingly attended, focusing on its inconveniences far more than the camaraderie.

Her friends, used to Amelia's easy-going ways, were amused by the shift. Yet, Amelia secretly feared her newfound contrarian attitude wasn't simply a quirky phase. It started to bleed into areas outside of work. When a movie her friends raved about became a huge box office hit, Amelia stubbornly put it at the bottom of her watchlist. Instead, she found herself seeking out obscure indie films, her counterculture taste becoming a point of pride.

Reactance

Amelia's behaviour is a perfect case study in psychological reactance. It's a complex human reaction against perceived encroachments on our freedom of choice. Essentially, anything that makes us feel like our freedoms or decision-making autonomy are being threatened generates a pushback — like a spring, the tighter it's squeezed, the more forceful the release.

Reactance has several key elements:

- **Threat to Choice:** This can be explicit (strict rules, directives) or subtle (social pressure, aggressively persuasive sales pitches).

- **Feeling Cornered:** The key emotional sensation is feeling like a behavioural freedom is being taken away, making us want to reclaim that freedom.

- **Backlash Behaviour:** This rebellion might be a rejection of the suggestion we object to or finding another way to restore our sense of freedom – the more forbidden it feels, the more tempting the alternate option.

From a psychological standpoint, it's about self-determination. Humans have a fundamental need to feel a sense of agency over their lives. When this is threatened, reactance is a knee-jerk defence mechanism. Some individuals have a naturally higher propensity for reactance than others, which, as Amelia is discovering, can be both liberating and troublesome.

While 'teenage rebellion' might be the stereotypical example of reactance, it can surface throughout our lives:

- **Politics:** Aggressive campaign tactics against an opposing side can backfire, strengthening voter loyalty to the targeted candidate instead.

- **Public Health:** Heavy-handed mandates, particularly surrounding sensitive areas like bodily autonomy, can fuel greater resistance instead of compliance.

- **Parenting:** Overly strict parenting might, ironically, increase the likelihood of the undesired behaviour occurring as the child attempts to regain control.

- **Marketing:** Pushy sales pitches often turn potential customers away, as even a good product feels less desirable when we feel the choice is being forced.

For Amelia, this instinct to reclaim lost freedoms started colouring her decisions in both positive and negative ways:

Positive:

- **Rediscovering Genuine Interests:** Resisting popular trends led her to uncover artistic niches (those obscure films) and new hobbies that aligned with her unique preferences.

- **Increased Self-Awareness:** Feeling cornered pushed her to identify the 'control triggers' that ignited her defiant impulse, giving her more self-insight.

- **Questioning Social Norms:** Reactance can spur an urge to explore the 'why' behind accepted routines, sometimes paving the way for positive change or individual liberation.

Negative:

- **Stubborn Contrarianism:** Pushing back became almost automatic, even when suggestions didn't pose a genuine threat to her choices.

- **Missed Opportunities:** Resisting advice at work meant ignoring potentially helpful tips simply because of their slightly condescending delivery.

- **Strained Relationships:** Friends grew cautious when excitedly recommending things, knowing Amelia might take an oppositional stance simply out of principle.

The key problem was her reactance becoming reactive. Instead of carefully choosing her battles to obtain genuine freedom, it spiralled into an almost subconscious reflex – defiance for defiance's sake. While resisting manipulation is valid, resisting any and all external nudges was taking its toll, replacing freethinking with reflexive opposition.

Sometimes, defiance against a 'push' in one direction creates unforeseen results:

- **The Banned Book Phenomenon:** Banning literature for controversial content has a long history of backfiring, with the forbidden materials often skyrocketing to bestseller status thanks to heightened curiosity and the feeling of rebellion buying it bestows.

- **Heavy-Handed Public Health Campaigns:** Campaigns trying too hard to deter unhealthy behaviours (think aggressively worded anti-smoking slogans) might fuel rebellious instincts, especially in youthful audiences.

- **Forbidden Romance:** When we're told not to have a relationship because of the disapproval of those close to us or a restrictive environment, it can sometimes increase its appeal, fuelled by a rebellious craving for the unattainable.

Like so many psychological tendencies, reactance isn't inherently bad. However, unmanaged, it can derail relationships, impede good decision-making and rob us of genuine opportunities. Awareness is the first step, followed by some deliberate strategies:

- **Self-Observation:** Identify your triggers. Does specific language set off your defiance? When feeling 'told what to do', check in with yourself: is my freedom being genuinely threatened?

- **The Pause and Separate:** Feelings and reason sometimes collide in reactance. Taking space allows emotion to dissipate, giving your rational mind time to evaluate the situation objectively.

- **Restoring Choice:** Sometimes, a tweak in communication style can lessen reactance. Being given options instead of direct orders can help us to regain a sense of autonomy.

- **Seeking the 'Why':** Explore your reaction instead of instantly suppressing it. It might hold insights about areas where you do need to stand firm and assert your preferences.

Questions for Self-Reflection

Do you recognize a bit of Amelia in yourself? Perhaps, on a smaller scale, her contrarian impulse mirrors internal battles we all face?

1. **The Weight of Obligation:** Does 'should' ignite 'shouldn't'? Do tasks lose appeal the moment they become obligations?

2. **The Reverse Trendsetter:** Is deciding solely in opposition to 'what everyone else is doing' driving your choices? Do you feel an urge to like what others dislike?

3. **What's Truly at Stake?** When feeling resistance, ask yourself what freedom is truly threatened. Is it the choice itself or simply how the choice is being presented?

4. **Gains or Losses:** Do your rebellions serve you? Sometimes, defiance fuels positive change. Ask yourself whether your pushback is driven by genuine values or the mere instinct to rebel?

5. **Identifying Where Choice Is Essential:** Recognizing our need for control helps us identify the areas where exerting independent judgment is critical to avoid a power struggle in situations where it matters less.

XLV. THE SPOTLIGHT EFFECT

Under the Microscope

Sarah had long been the epitome of a prudent investor. Her approach to investing was nothing short of meticulous – each decision backed by rigorous research, each move a testament to her deep understanding of the markets. Over the years, her strategy paid off, culminating in a portfolio that was both diversified and prosperous. Yet, the financial world is as unforgiving as it is rewarding, and even the most seasoned investors are not immune to its trials. For Sarah, what began as a series of minor setbacks soon burgeoned into a crisis of confidence that shook the very foundations of her investing philosophy.

As she settled into her home office to conduct her routine portfolio review, an activity that had once been a source of pride and satisfaction, Sarah was met with an unfamiliar sense of foreboding. The glow of her computer screen, once a reassuring beacon of clarity, now felt like a harsh spotlight, casting her every decision into sharp relief. It was as though an audience of unseen critics had taken up residence in her mind, scrutinizing her every move with an unsparing eye.

With each scroll through her portfolio, Sarah's imagination conjured vivid scenarios of judgment and scepticism. She envisioned seasoned financial experts shaking their heads in distaste at her choices, her peers whispering about her apparent missteps and an abstract audience questioning her competence. This imagined chorus of disapproval turned the simple act of reviewing her investments into an ordeal, magnifying the significance of every market fluctuation and amplifying her self-doubt.

The small upsets in her portfolio, typical of the ebb and flow of the financial markets, now loomed large in Sarah's mind. Each dip in stock performance was interpreted not as a normal part of investing but as a glaring indictment of her abilities. The rational, analytical part of her brain, which had guided her to success, was now overshadowed by a paralyzing fear of judgment. This fear distorted her perception, making her believe that her every move was being watched and critiqued with an intensity that far exceeded reality.

This phenomenon, known as the spotlight effect, describes the tendency to overestimate the extent to which our actions and appearance are noted by others. In Sarah's case, it had insidiously woven itself into her investing process, transforming it from a disciplined exercise in financial planning into a source of anxiety and self-doubt. It had tricked her into believing that her every decision was under a microscope, subject to the relentless scrutiny of an audience that, in reality, did not exist.

Confronted with this realization, Sarah understood that regaining her confidence would require her to confront the spotlight effect head-on. She began by reminding herself that the imagined audience of critics was a construct of her own making, their judgments a reflection of her insecurities rather than any objective reality. She revisited the principles that had guided her to success, focusing on the long-term strategy rather than the short-term fluctuations that had so easily rattled her.

Gradually, Sarah learned to silence the imaginary critics, to turn down the intensity of the spotlight she had cast upon herself. She returned to her research and analysis with renewed vigour, armed with the knowledge that her true audience was simply her future self, for whom she was diligently building a foundation of financial security. By recognizing and addressing the spotlight effect, Sarah not only reclaimed her confidence as an investor but also rediscovered the joy and satisfaction in the process of investing itself.

The Spotlight Effect

The spotlight effect is a cognitive distortion where individuals believe their actions, appearance and words are being observed and judged more closely by others than they actually are. This effect, deeply ingrained in human psychology, often leads to an inflated sense of self-consciousness. It's a phenomenon that stretches across various aspects of life, including social interactions and professional environments, with particular relevance to the high-stakes world of finance and investing.

The spotlight effect was first identified and named by social psychologists Thomas Gilovich, Victoria Medvec and Kenneth Savitsky. Their research demonstrated that people often overestimate the extent to which their actions and appearance are noted by others, a result of the natural egocentric bias in human cognition. This bias leads us to project our awareness onto others, assuming they share our focus on our faults and missteps.

Several underlying mechanisms contribute to the spotlight effect:

- **Egocentrism:** At its core, the spotlight effect is driven by an egocentric bias, where individuals struggle to differentiate between their awareness of themselves and that of others. This results in overestimating the visibility of one's own actions or appearance.

- **Social Anxiety:** For many, especially those prone to social anxiety, the spotlight effect is intensified by fears of negative evaluation, leading to heightened self-consciousness and avoidance behaviour.

- **Self-Consciousness:** High levels of private and public self-consciousness can amplify the effect, making individuals more acutely aware of how they believe they are perceived by others.

In the realm of finance and investing, the spotlight effect can have significant implications:

- **Fear of Judgment:** Investors may avoid sound investment opportunities due to fear of judgment for potential losses, leading to overly conservative or herd-following behaviours.

- **Short-Term Focus:** Concern over the perceived judgment of others can shift an investor's focus from long-term strategies to short-term gains, undermining the potential for higher long-term returns.

- **Decision Paralysis:** The exaggerated fear of scrutiny and criticism can lead to decision paralysis, where the fear of making the wrong decision prevents any decision at all.

Addressing the spotlight effect requires both awareness of its influence and deliberate strategies to counteract its effects:

- **Perspective Taking:** Actively reminding oneself that others are likely more focused on their own affairs can help reduce the perceived intensity of scrutiny.

- **Cognitive Behavioural Techniques:** Strategies such as cognitive restructuring can help challenge and change exaggerated beliefs about being in the spotlight.

- **Social Skills Training:** For those whose spotlight effect is tied to social anxiety, developing stronger social skills and confidence can reduce the intensity of perceived judgment.

The spotlight effect reveals the complex interplay between self-perception, social cognition and behaviour. By understanding and actively managing this cognitive bias, individuals can navigate social and professional environments, including the financial market, with greater confidence and clarity. Recognizing that our fears of judgment are often exaggerated can liberate us from the constraints of imagined scrutiny, enabling more rational decision-making and authentic interactions.

Questions for Self-Reflection

The crucial first step in managing the spotlight effect is identifying its presence in your own investment practice. Consider these introspective questions:

1. **How do you react to losses?** Do setbacks, even minor ones, disproportionately chip away at your confidence and create a debilitating fear of making additional 'mistakes'? Is your emotional response greater than the situation warrants?

2. **Do you perceive judgment?** When an investment underperforms, do you internalize it as a reflection of your abilities, imagining that colleagues, acquaintances or even financial media figures are critiquing your every decision?

3. **Are you overly focused on the opinions of others?** Do you place greater weight on external validation or the fleeting hot takes of commentators than on your own disciplined research and well-formulated investment plan?

4. **Do you find yourself conforming?** In an attempt to shield yourself from perceived judgment, do you fall into the trap of mimicking mainstream trends and abandoning your independent investment strategies?

5. **Are you losing your long-term focus?** Are recent setbacks hindering your ability to adhere to your long-term investment goals? Are you making short-sighted decisions influenced by anxiety rather than a sound, strategic vision?

XLVI. THE BYSTANDER EFFECT

Frozen by Indecision

Mark's journey into the world of stock investing had always been marked by a careful, deliberate approach. Over the years, he had managed to assemble a portfolio that reflected his conservative investment style, balancing the reliability of steady index funds with the potential of a select few companies. This methodical strategy served him well, allowing him to navigate the markets with a sense of security and measured optimism.

However, the emergence of a high-growth tech stock, surrounded by a whirlwind of media attention and praise from analysts, presented a new kind of challenge for Mark. The stock was being touted as a game-changer, a beacon of innovation with the potential to redefine the industry. The fervour surrounding it was palpable, with articles and analyst reports predicting unprecedented growth. This buzz created an irresistible allure, tapping into Mark's fear of missing out (FOMO) on what was being hailed as a once-in-a-lifetime investment opportunity.

Yet, amidst the excitement, a seed of doubt took root in Mark's mind. The company's valuation, inflated by the buzz, seemed disconnected from its fundamentals. Moreover, whispers of unsustainable business practices began to emerge on various financial forums, casting a shadow over the glowing narratives. Mark found himself caught in a maze of conflicting information, with each analyst offering a radically different perspective on the stock's future and countless online personalities contributing to an ever-growing cacophony of opinions.

The more Mark delved into this sea of contradictions, the more elusive his path forward became. It was as if every investor and commentator had access to some critical piece of the puzzle that he was missing. The flood of data was overwhelming; instead of guiding his decision, it only served to heighten his indecision. Mark found himself unable to act, paralyzed by the fear of making the wrong choice. This paralysis was not merely a symptom of information overload but a manifestation of the bystander effect.

Traditionally understood in the context of social psychology, the bystander effect posits that individuals are less likely to take action or intervene in an emergency when others are present. In Mark's case, this psychological phenomenon manifested as an inability to make an investment decision, driven by the perception that a multitude of other informed investors and experts 'present' in the digital realm somehow absolved him of the need to act decisively.

Confronted with this realization, Mark recognized that overcoming his paralysis would require not just filtering the noise but also acknowledging the psychological barriers that kept him from acting. He began to understand that the collective wisdom of the market could not replace his own judgment and that the responsibility to make informed decisions rested solely on his shoulders.

To combat the bystander effect and regain his sense of agency, Mark adopted a more structured approach to his research, focusing on credible sources and fundamental analysis rather than getting swept up in speculative hype. He set clear criteria for his investments, based on risk tolerance and long-term goals, and he committed to a decision-making process that prioritized these standards over the fluctuating sentiment of the crowd.

Through this journey, Mark learned that in the world of investing, as in life, the presence of others' opinions and actions should not deter one from trusting their own judgment and making decisions that align with their values and objectives. By recognizing and addressing the bystander effect, Mark not only regained his confidence as an investor but also reinforced his commitment to a thoughtful, independent approach to building his portfolio.

The Bystander Effect

As we've seen, the bystander effect isn't only about aiding strangers in physical emergencies. It also influences financial decision-making, especially in this hyper-connected digital age where our awareness of what everyone else is doing and saying is heightened. Here's how the core elements of the bystander effect translate to the investment context:

- **Diffusion of Responsibility:** With countless financial news sources, expert opinions and social media commentary just a few clicks away, we have the illusion that someone else always has superior knowledge or better access to analysis. We assume that due diligence, or even minimal diligence, is being conducted elsewhere, reducing our sense of responsibility in fully grasping a particular investment or market trend ('If it were a truly bad investment, surely someone else would be sounding the alarm').

- **Fear of Social Judgement:** In an environment saturated with performance boasts and tales of lucrative trades, it's natural to want to avoid 'rocking the boat'. Expressing scepticism, asking critical questions or going against herd mentality can come with its own form of social risk. Investors may self-censor their doubts, fearing ridicule or accusations of insufficient competence from fellow investors, analysts or the online financial community ('If I question this hot stock, I'll just look like I don't know what I'm doing').

- **Ambiguity and Information Overload:** Modern markets are awash with complex data, diverse perspectives and an overwhelming volume of real-time updates. Investors are more likely to fall prey to inaction if they lack confidence sorting through conflicting information or if there is no single, obviously 'correct' decision based on available data ('So many analysts are bullish, yet there's this negative report... It's impossible to know who's right!').

- **Pluralistic Ignorance:** Investors, especially those newer to the field, instinctively look to others to gauge market sentiment and determine acceptable risk levels. When everyone else seems to favour a particular asset class, stock or trend, individuals assume these actions reflect collective wisdom. Their own well-founded worries may be downplayed for fear of ignoring everyone's enthusiasm ('Everyone is buying into crypto... I'm not sure, but maybe I'm too old-fashioned and just don't get it').

The bystander effect creates the following potential pitfalls for investors:

- **Herd Mentality:** When independent evaluation is hampered by doubt and our perception of the crowd's expertise, investors can be driven towards popular stocks or trendy investment strategies without conducting sufficient research. This risks misaligned investments and vulnerability when market bubbles burst.

- **Missed Opportunities:** While blindly following the herd is dangerous, so is constant second-guessing. Overreliance on the consensus or a paralyzing fear of acting decisively can lead to lost opportunities to enter favourable positions or sell a failing investment before more extensive losses are incurred.

- **Emotional Trading and Market Noise:** As feelings of confusion and isolation mount due to the bystander effect, emotional decision-making often takes over. Fear and greed can be amplified when investors believe they lack the same inside knowledge as those 'in the know'. This can result in panic selling, chasing hyped-up assets and impulsive moves driven by social pressure rather than logic.

- **Erosion of Individual Learning:** Outsourcing crucial investment decisions to the perceived collective intelligence of the market hinders skill development. True investor acumen is derived from critical thinking, informed risk assessment and continuous learning – factors stifled by a heavy reliance on external validation.

Questions for Self-Reflection

We're all wired with certain social instincts, making susceptibility to the bystander effect entirely natural. Recognizing how it manifests in an investment context is the first step towards more autonomous decision-making. Consider these self-reflective questions:

1. **Whose Opinions Do You Rely On?** Do you tend to fixate on the predictions of certain pundits, popular personalities or specific 'gurus'? Have you neglected to examine potential contrarian views from sources outside your usual information channels?

2. **Are You a 'Doer' or a 'Watcher'?** Do you find yourself reading opinions and market analysis but hesitating to apply that knowledge within your portfolio? Are you plagued by analysis paralysis, struggling to translate research into active decisions?

3. **What Are Your Go-To Information Sources?** Do you primarily get your financial news and investment ideas from mainstream outlets, social media personalities or perhaps friends and family? Do you actively seek out diverse and sometimes contradictory viewpoints to challenge your existing assumptions and counteract potential information bubbles?

4. **Do You Have a Clear Investment Philosophy?** Have you articulated your core principles regarding risk tolerance, diversification, investment timelines and the weight you place on fundamentals vs market sentiment? A defined philosophy

acts as an anchor when the bystander effect threatens to throw your decision-making off course.

5. **Are You Comfortable with 'Missing Out'?** Is your main worry FOMO (fear of missing out) on the next big thing? If so, are you more likely to override your usual research process and sound judgment in the hope of catching a rapidly moving wave of speculation? Remember, investment success is often about patience and discipline as much as it is about finding the next home run.

XLVII. AUTHORITY BIAS

The Weight of Titles

Sarah's recent promotion to project manager was a milestone she had eagerly anticipated, marking the culmination of years of dedication and hard work within her company. With a head brimming with innovative ideas and a heart set on making a significant impact, she approached her first major assignment with a mix of enthusiasm and ambition. The task at hand was a challenging one – a comprehensive redesign of a key product in the company's portfolio. Sarah saw this as a golden opportunity to leave her mark by implementing fresh strategies and creative approaches that could redefine the project's trajectory.

As preparations for the redesign got underway, Sarah convened a series of brainstorming sessions aimed at harnessing the collective creativity and expertise of her team. It was during one of these collaborative meetings that Dr. Johnson, a senior developer with years of experience and a respected authority in the field, proposed a technical approach grounded in traditional methodologies. Dr. Johnson spoke with the conviction of someone who had navigated similar projects before, confidently asserting that his approach had been time-tested and proven to yield reliable results.

Sarah, while initially keen to infuse the project with new and innovative solutions, found herself increasingly swayed by Dr. Johnson's assertive demeanour and the weight of his experience. Despite an underlying sense of unease about the compatibility of his proposed method with the dynamic nature of the project, she struggled to voice her reservations. The aura of authority that Dr. Johnson projected exerted a subtle yet powerful influence, leading Sarah to question her own instincts and ideas.

In a decision that would later come to haunt her, Sarah chose to sideline her creative vision in favour of the path laid out by Dr. Johnson. She rationalized this choice as deference to his expertise, convincing herself that it was the safer, more prudent route to ensuring project success.

However, the project launch revealed a different reality. The approach, while technically sound, failed to resonate with the target audience and did not deliver the anticipated impact. The product's redesign, constrained by conventional methodologies, lacked the innovative edge Sarah had initially envisioned.

In the aftermath of the launch, Sarah embarked on a period of introspection, seeking to understand the missteps that led to this lacklustre outcome. It was through this reflective process that she encountered the concept of authority bias – the tendency to attribute greater accuracy and value to the opinions of an authority figure, often at the expense of one's own judgment and innovative potential.

This realization was a turning point for Sarah. She recognized that her deference to Dr. Johnson, while rooted in respect, had inadvertently stifled her own creative contributions. It had clouded her decision-making, leading her to forgo a potentially groundbreaking approach in favour of a more traditional and less appropriate solution.

Determined to learn from this experience, Sarah resolved to strike a balance between valuing the insights of experienced colleagues and trusting her own innovative instincts. She understood now that effective leadership was not just about making decisions but about fostering an environment where diverse ideas and approaches could coexist and complement each other.

As Sarah looked forward to leading future projects, she did so with a renewed sense of confidence in her ability to navigate the complexities of authority bias. This experience, though challenging, had given her a deeper understanding of her strengths as a leader and the importance of advocating for her vision while remaining open to the wisdom of others.

Authority Bias

Authority bias describes our tendency to give greater weight to the opinions, instructions and influence of authority figures. Whether it's a boss, a doctor, someone with an important title or simply someone who acts in a confident, assertive manner, we often feel compelled to accept their input over our own or that of those without this perceived status.

Let's examine why we're vulnerable to this bias with some guiding questions:

- **Early Conditioning:** From childhood, we're socialized to follow rules and obey figures in positions of power. Reflect on these ingrained patterns. Can you trace how they may unconsciously influence your current responses to perceived authority?

- **Mental Shortcuts:** We frequently default to authority as a cognitive shortcut. Relying on experts saves time and mental energy, especially in unfamiliar situations. But can you spot when this becomes excessive, allowing expertise in one area to create a halo effect?

- **Fear of the Unknown:** When unsure, seeking guidance from experts offers reassurance. Do you fall back on perceived authority to avoid the discomfort of independent decision-making? Does this sometimes prevent critical evaluation?

While respecting expertise is a wise course of action in many situations, unchecked authority bias can lead to undesirable outcomes. Sarah's stalled project demonstrates this. Here are some examples using other contexts:

- **Medical Malpractice:** A doctor may misdiagnose a patient who hesitates to ask questions because they perceive the doctor as the ultimate authority on the subject.

- **Unjust Convictions:** Jurors may prioritize a forensic expert's testimony over contradictory evidence, due to the perceived authority conferred by their specialized title and professional role.

- **Business Blunders:** CEOs, under pressure to succeed, may stifle dissenting voices who point out flaws in an ambitious plan. The team may simply accept this behaviour because they are an authority figure.

The very fact that Sarah recognized her mistake was the first step towards mitigating authority bias. Let's consider other strategies to combat its influence:

- **Seeking Multiple Perspectives:** Can you consciously expand your sources of information before making a decision? Are you including varied viewpoints beyond the loudest or most prominent authority figures?

- **Devil's Advocate:** Could you assign a designated 'questioner' in a group setting to respectfully challenge ideas? This can counter groupthink and unchecked acceptance of an authority figure's suggestions.

- **Voicing Your Concerns:** Can you muster the courage to speak up even when the other person holds greater status? When done politely and rationally, presenting well-articulated counter-arguments can lead to stronger outcomes.

We must emphasize that expertise matters! Trusting credible, reputable sources with a proven track record is vital. The key lies in recognizing when 'authority' overrides sound judgment. This awareness gives us greater ownership of our decision-making and ensures we make more well-rounded and informed evaluations. Remember that, sometimes, true expertise can come from your own critical thinking and intuition.

Questions for Self-Reflection

1. **Are You a People Pleaser?** Do you find yourself easily going along with decisions proposed by superiors or individuals in authority to avoid confrontation or gain their approval?

Recognizing our internal need for validation can help us identify blind spots.

2. **Expertise vs Assumption:** Do you have a tendency to assume that experts are infallible and possess knowledge in areas outside their primary specialization? Do titles or credentials inadvertently grant undeserved credibility across topics?

3. **Challenging Your Inner Voice:** When an authority figure suggests something counter to your beliefs or instincts, do you have an internal dialogue to evaluate the idea rather than automatically dismissing your own thinking?

4. **Your Past Mistakes:** Can you recall a time when blindly following an authority figure led to an error or undesirable outcome? Looking back, what warning signs did you miss, and how can you avoid making similar mistakes in the future?

5. **Comfort Zone Bias:** Does relying on authority figures provide a sense of comfort and reduce personal accountability for outcomes? Does this sometimes lead to passively accepting ideas rather than engaging your own critical thinking?

XLVIII. EGOCENTRIC BIAS

The Portfolio Paradox

Elena was a seasoned investment adviser whose reputation lay in thoughtfully predicting the market and making bespoke investment strategies for clients. The returns across her portfolio were impressive and clearly above the market average, which she most often attributed to sharp analysis and instincts that could almost be considered genetic. But there were some clients of hers that didn't fully appreciate her talents. Marcus was a very conservative investor; at times, too much so. His approach always seemed to be at odds with hers, which tended to be rather aggressive. In fact, however much success she had, Elena failed to do one thing: convince Marcus to make more daring investments. As evidence, he would constantly bring up a few cases where he listened to her and returned home with fewer profits than expected.

Convinced that her method was better, Elena decided to review her investment strategies over time and show him how effective they were, beyond reasonable doubt. But, as she ran through the analysis, and quite unexpectedly, something revealed itself. It was true that, in general, she had done well for herself, but further scrutiny yielded another story. It wasn't as unblemished a record as she recollected. Several investments that she had recommended confidently had underperformed, while some that she warned against – including certain stocks which Marcus had insisted upon retaining – were doing reasonably well, if not exceptionally. That felt odd. Elena prided herself on being objective and always using her analytical mind. So, why did her memories of successful and unsuccessful investments get so warped?

Egocentric Bias

Egocentric bias is a cognitive distortion that leads individuals to rely excessively on their own perspective and attributes, often at the expense of more objective analysis. This bias manifests in various ways, including overemphasizing one's contributions to a group effort or recalling past events in a manner that favours one's own role or decisions.

Egocentric bias is rooted in the way humans process information and memories. It reflects our innate tendency to view the world from our own perspective, which can lead to a skewed interpretation of events and decisions. This bias is closely related to concepts like the self-serving bias, where individuals attribute positive outcomes to their own actions and negative outcomes to external factors.

One of the primary psychological mechanisms behind egocentric bias is memory reconstruction. Our memories are not static records but are reconstructed each time we recall them. This reconstruction process is influenced by our current beliefs, feelings and self-perception, leading to a biased recall of past events that aligns with our self-image.

Another mechanism at work is the theory of mind – our ability to attribute mental states to ourselves and others. Egocentric bias can occur when we fail to fully account for others' perspectives, leading to an overreliance on our own viewpoint.

In the realm of professional investing, egocentric bias can have significant implications.

- **Overestimation of Our Contributions:** Investors may overestimate their contribution to successful outcomes while downplaying their role in failures. This bias can lead to an inflated sense of one's investing acumen, as seen in Elena's initial assessment of her performance.
- **Faulty Risk Assessment and Decision-Making:** An investor might remember their successful risk-taking decisions more vividly than their cautious decisions that averted losses, leading to a distorted perception of their risk tolerance and decision-making skills.
- **Hinders Learning and Adaptation:** By selectively recalling investment successes, professionals might fail to accurately analyse and learn from past decisions, potentially repeating mistakes or missing opportunities for improvement.

Here are some ideas for mitigating egocentric bias:

- **Seek Objective Feedback:** Regularly consult with peers or mentors who can provide unbiased perspectives on your decisions and performance. External feedback can help counterbalance our natural inclination to view our actions in a disproportionately positive light.
- **Maintain a Decision Journal:** Keep a detailed record of investment decisions, including the rationale and the expected and actual results. This practice encourages accountability and

provides a more objective basis for evaluating decision-making processes and outcomes.

- **Embrace Diverse Perspectives:** Actively seek out and consider viewpoints different from your own. Exposure to a range of perspectives can challenge egocentric assumptions and facilitate a more balanced understanding of investment decisions.

- **Conduct Regular Performance Reviews:** Implement systematic and comprehensive reviews of your investment performance using standardized metrics and methodologies that will help you to assess success and failure objectively.

- **Practice Mindfulness and Self-Reflection:** Engage in practices that enhance self-awareness and the ability to critique one's own thoughts and actions without bias. Mindfulness can help us recognize when egocentric bias is influencing decision-making.

Questions for Self-Reflection

1. **Impact of Personal Experiences:** How have my personal experiences and successes shaped my investment decisions, and could they be leading me to overlook broader market indicators or alternative strategies?

2. **Seeking and Incorporating Contradictory Information:** When making investment decisions, do I actively seek out information that contradicts my current beliefs or strategies? How do I incorporate this into my decision-making process?

3. **Evaluating the Basis of Investment Confidence:** Can I identify instances where my confidence in my investment judgment was based more on past successes than on a thorough analysis of the current market conditions?

4. **Balancing Personal Insight with Market Data:** How do I balance my personal insights and experiences with objective market data and analysis in my investment strategy?

5. **Openness to Diverse Perspectives:** What steps can I take to ensure that I remain open to diverse investment perspectives and avoid letting my personal experiences unduly influence my investment decisions?

XLIX. STATUS QUO BIAS

The Comfort of Familiar Waters

Marta Sullivan had built her reputation in the world of finance on the bedrock of a conservative investment strategy that prized stability over speculation. For years, her approach, centred around blue-chip stocks and high-grade bonds, had been the compass guiding her clients through the tumultuous seas of the market. This strategy had not only earned her respect within the investment firm but had also fostered a deep sense of trust with her clientele, who valued the predictable, though modest, returns on their investments.

However, the winds of change were blowing through the financial markets. Emerging sectors, powered by technological innovations and shifting consumer behaviours, began to reshape the investment landscape. These alternative investments started to show remarkable returns, outshining the traditional stalwarts of Marta's portfolio. These changes did not go unnoticed within her firm. Colleagues, buoyed by this potential, advocated for a re-evaluation of the firm's investment strategy so as to embrace these new opportunities.

Marta, however, found herself at a crossroads. Her career had been defined by a cautious approach that eschewed the volatile for the dependable. The very thought of venturing into less familiar territory, with its unpredictable risks and outcomes, was antithetical to her philosophy. Despite the compelling arguments and the allure of higher returns, she hesitated, preferring the safety of the known.

As time marched on, the consequences of Marta's reluctance began to manifest. The portfolios she managed, once paragons of stability and steady growth, started to show signs of stagnation. Comparisons with her peers, who had pivoted to embrace the changing market dynamics, highlighted the growing disparity. Their portfolios not only weathered market fluctuations but also capitalized on them, achieving substantial growth.

This realization struck Marta with force. The strategy that had served her and her clients so well in a different era was now a relic of the past, ill-suited to navigating the new financial landscape. The steadfastness that had been her hallmark was, in this new context, a limitation. She understood that her commitment to her clients was not just to preserve their wealth but to grow it – to seek out the best opportunities for their investments, even if it meant stepping outside her comfort zone.

Emboldened by this insight, Marta began the process of transformation. She immersed herself in the study of emerging sectors, seeking to understand the nuances of these new markets and the nature of the risks involved. She engaged with her colleagues, leveraging their insight to reshape her investment philosophy. Gradually, her portfolio began to reflect this evolution, incorporating a mix of traditional stability and targeted, strategic risk-taking.

This shift was not without its challenges. Each decision was a balancing act between potential and prudence, requiring a level of vigilance and adaptability that was new to Marta. Yet, with each success, her confidence grew. Her clients, seeing the renewed vigour and growth in their portfolios, rallied to her side, their trust in her expertise deepened by her willingness to adapt for their benefit.

Marta's journey was a testament to the importance of flexibility in the face of change. It underscored the reality that in the dynamic world of investment, the greatest risk often lies in adherence to the status quo. By embracing change and confronting uncertainty, Marta not only revitalized her career but also reaffirmed her commitment to her clients, guiding them with renewed energy towards a prosperous future.

Status Quo Bias

This cognitive bias describes the preference to keep things in their current state, while viewing any change as a potential risk or opportunity for loss. It can cause individuals and institutions to prefer the familiar and resist change, even when the evidence suggests that a different course of action would be better.

Status quo bias is closely related to loss aversion and the endowment effect, where individuals tend to overvalue what they currently have and underestimate the benefits of change. It is also influenced by effort justification, where people rationalize their past choices, and the sunk cost fallacy, where past investments influence future decisions.

For investors like Marta, status quo bias can lead to a reluctance to diversify portfolios or to adopt new investment strategies that align with the evolution of the market. This bias can result in missed opportunities and potential underperformance. It can also make investors stick with underperforming assets or strategies simply because they are accustomed to them.

Investors can overcome status quo bias in the following ways:

- **Periodic Review:** Regularly reviewing investment strategies and holdings with an eye on objective performance metrics will encourage a change of tactics when it's necessary.

- **Seeking External Input:** Consulting with outside experts who can provide a fresh perspective on the portfolio will reveal when you are clinging to the status quo.

- **Flexibility in Planning:** Building flexibility into investment plans will allow you to more easily adapt to changing market conditions.

Questions for Self-Reflection

1. **Reviewing for Bias:** When was the last time you reviewed your investment strategy? Have you avoided changes due to the comfort of familiarity?

2. **Portfolio Impact:** Can you identify decisions where you may have favoured the status quo due to an aversion to loss or effort justification? How might those decisions have impacted your portfolio's performance?

3. **The Sunk Cost Fallacy:** Reflect on a situation where you decided to maintain an underperforming asset. Was this decision influenced by the amount of time or money you had already invested in it?

4. **Valuing External Perspectives:** How often do you seek external advice on your investment strategy? Could an outside perspective help you challenge your own status quo bias?

5. **Adapting Strategy to Address Market Changes:** Consider a past instance where a change in the market required a shift in strategy. How did you respond, and what were the outcomes of that decision?

L. THE OSTRICH EFFECT

Ignoring the Coming Storm

Emily was well-aware of market cycles, understanding that ups and downs were part of the investment journey. However, as the markets began to show signs of a significant downturn, Emily found herself increasingly reluctant to review her portfolio. The daily news was awash with reports of economic uncertainty, and each headline seemed to herald worsening conditions.

At first, Emily's decision to avoid checking her investments felt like a relief. By not seeing the losses, she shielded herself from the immediate emotional discomfort of witnessing her portfolio's decline. This avoidance became a pattern, with Emily rationalizing that if she didn't look, the problem didn't exist, or at the very least, it wasn't hers to contend with just yet.

However, as the downturn became prolonged, Emily's friends and family began discussing their strategies for managing their investments through the volatility. Some spoke of rebalancing their portfolios, and others of seizing the opportunity to buy undervalued stocks, while a few talked about the importance of staying the course, trusting in their long-term investment strategies.

Hearing these conversations, Emily realized that her avoidance had a cost. While she had been ignoring her portfolio, she had missed opportunities to make informed decisions that could have mitigated her losses or even positioned her for greater long-term gains. The comfort provided by the ostrich effect was fleeting, and in its place, Emily found a growing sense of unease about the potential state of her investments.

Determined to confront the reality she had been avoiding, Emily finally reviewed her portfolio. As expected, there were losses, some of which were significant. However, with the market's downturn now fully in view, Emily began to see opportunities for action. She recognized that some assets in her portfolio were well-positioned for recovery, while others might benefit from being sold or rebalanced. What had once seemed an insurmountable challenge now appeared as a series of manageable decisions.

Through this experience, Emily learned a critical lesson. While avoiding negative and uncomfortable information – the ostrich effect – might provide temporary emotional relief, it also hinders our ability to make proactive, informed decisions. By choosing to face her portfolio, Emily not only regained control over her investment strategy but also overcame the paralysis that had prevented her from acting in her best financial interests.

The Ostrich Effect

The ostrich effect, a term inspired by the myth that ostriches bury their heads in the sand to avoid danger, refers to the cognitive bias wherein investors choose to ignore negative financial information when it feels uncomfortable to face. This effect is particularly observed during periods of market volatility or downturn, where the instinct to avoid distressing news leads individuals to steer clear of checking their investment portfolios or financial statements. The underlying motivation is a desire to evade the psychological discomfort associated with acknowledging financial losses or unfavourable market conditions.

The ostrich effect is rooted in our aversion to loss and negative emotions. Facing financial losses can trigger stress, anxiety and a sense of failure – emotions that individuals naturally wish to avoid. By not monitoring their investments during downturns, investors temporarily shield themselves from these negative feelings. However, this avoidance behaviour is counterproductive as it can lead to missed opportunities for corrective action, such as rebalancing the portfolio, selling off underperforming assets or buying undervalued stocks that may rebound. Additionally, this effect can hinder investors from developing a comprehensive understanding of market dynamics and their personal risk tolerance, both of which are essential components of effective investment strategy.

Overcoming the ostrich effect involves acknowledging its presence and understanding the value of staying informed, even in the face of adverse financial news. Strategies to mitigate this bias include setting regular intervals for portfolio review, regardless of market conditions, and adopting a long-term perspective on investments to reduce the emotional impact of short-term volatility. Engaging with a financial advisor for objective advice and emotional support can also help investors navigate periods of uncertainty without resorting to avoidance behaviours.

While primarily discussed in the context of financial decision-making, the ostrich effect has broader implications for how individuals deal with negative information or feedback in other aspects of life. Whether in personal health, career development or relationships, the tendency to ignore unpleasant realities can hinder growth, problem-solving and the ability to make proactive changes.

In summary, the ostrich effect underscores the complex interplay between psychology and financial decision-making. By recognizing and addressing this bias, investors can enhance their resilience against market volatility, make more informed decisions, and ultimately, improve their financial well-being.

Questions for Self-Reflection

1. **Confronting Financial Realities:** Have there been times when you avoided looking at your investments or financial statements due to fear of bad news? What was the outcome?

2. **The Benefits of Facing the Facts Early On:** Reflecting on past financial decisions, can you identify moments when facing the facts sooner might have led to better outcomes?

3. **Building a Routine for Financial Review:** How can you create a habit of regularly reviewing your financial situation, even when you suspect the news might not be good?

4. **Emotional Resilience:** In what ways can you prepare yourself emotionally to face financial downturns without resorting to avoidance?

5. **Learning from the Ostrich Effect:** How might understanding and acknowledging the ostrich effect change your approach to financial planning and investment strategy moving forward?

CONCLUSION

As we arrive at the final pages of this exploration of the world of human behaviour, it's time to turn the lens inward and reflect on the journey we've embarked upon together. Throughout this book, we've navigated the complex terrain of cognitive, emotional and social biases that influence not only our investment decisions but also the myriad choices we face in our daily lives. By engaging with the questions for self-reflection posed in each chapter, you've taken a crucial step towards uncovering the subtle yet profound ways in which these biases can shape our thoughts and actions.

Now, I invite you to pause and consider the following: How did you find the experience of answering these questions for self-reflection? Were there moments of surprise or recognition as you identified biases in your own decision-making process? Perhaps you encountered resistance or discomfort when confronting certain biases that hit close to home. These reactions are not only natural but also incredibly valuable. They signify the beginning of increased self-awareness and a deeper understanding of the complex interplay between our minds and the decisions we make.

The journey towards understanding and mitigating our biases does not have a final destination. Rather, it's a continuous process of learning and growth. It requires patience, humility and the willingness to question and challenge our assumptions and behaviours. As you reflect on your responses to the questions for self-reflection, I encourage you to consider whether you now feel more aware of the underlying reasons for your decisions. Has this heightened awareness prompted you to think differently about how you approach investment decisions or other aspects of your life?

This book aims to illuminate the path towards greater self-awareness and rational decision-making by fostering an understanding of the psychological biases that influence us. However, the true work begins with each individual's commitment to applying these insights in their daily lives. As you move forward, remember that awareness of our biases is the first step towards mastering them. By continuing to engage in self-reflection and seeking to understand the reasons behind our choices, we can better navigate the complexities of the financial markets and our personal lives.

FURTHER READING

Kahneman, Daniel. *Thinking, Fast and Slow.* Farrar, Straus and Giroux, 2011.

Thaler, Richard H. *Misbehaving: The Making of Behavioural Economics.* W. W. Norton & Company, 2015.

Tversky, Amos, and Daniel Kahneman. *Judgment under Uncertainty: Heuristics and Biases.* Cambridge University Press, 1982.

Shiller, Robert J. *Irrational Exuberance.* Princeton University Press, 2000.

Ariely, Dan. *Predictably Irrational: The Hidden Forces That Shape Our Decisions.* HarperCollins, 2008.

Montier, James. *Behavioural Investing: A Practitioner's Guide to Applying Behavioural Finance.* Wiley, 2007.

Shefrin, Hersh. *Beyond Greed and Fear: Understanding Behavioural Finance and the Psychology of Investing.* Oxford University Press, 2002.

Tversky, Amos, and Daniel Kahneman. *The Framing of Decisions and the Psychology of Choice.* **Science**, vol. 211, no. 4481, 1981, pp. 453-458.

Fama, Eugene F. *Efficient Capital Markets: A Review of Theory and Empirical Work.* **The Journal of Finance**, vol. 25, no. 2, 1970, pp. 383-417.

Thaler, Richard H., and Cass R. Sunstein. *Nudge: Improving Decisions About Health, Wealth, and Happiness.* Yale University Press, 2008.

Barberis, Nicholas, and Richard Thaler. *A Survey of Behavioural Finance.* In *Handbook of the Economics of Finance*, edited by G.M. Constantinides, M. Harris, and R. Stulz, Elsevier, 2003, pp. 1053-1128.

Kahneman, Daniel, and Amos Tversky. *Prospect Theory: An Analysis of Decision under Risk.* **Econometrica**, vol. 47, no. 2, 1979, pp. 263-291.

Shleifer, Andrei. *Inefficient Markets: An Introduction to Behavioural Finance.* Oxford University Press, 2000.

De Bondt, Werner F.M., and Richard H. Thaler. *Does the Stock Market Overreact?* **The Journal of Finance**, vol. 40, no. 3, 1985, pp. 793-805.

Nofsinger, John R. *The Psychology of Investing.* Routledge, 2023.

Advances in Behavioural Finance, edited by Richard H. Thaler. Princeton University Press, 2005.

Journal of Behavioural Finance – A journal dedicated to the study of behavioural aspects of financial theory and practice.

www.ingramcontent.com/pod-product-compliance
Lightning Source LLC
Chambersburg PA
CBHW050048230526
45470CB00004B/1442